San Diego
Official Guidebook

2020

Maria Desiderata Montana

(sandiegofoodfinds.com)

Dedication

To my loyal followers who have made San Diego Food Finds a top online food guide in America's Finest City.

Table of Contents

About the Author

Maria Desiderata Montana is the publisher of the award-winning and top online food guide San Diego Food Finds (sandiegofoodfinds.com). She is also a nationally published and award-winning author, food and wine journalist and photographer.

Maria is the author of Food Lovers' Guide to San Diego (Globe Pequot Press), San Diego Chef's Table: Extraordinary Recipes From America's Finest City (Lyons Press), San Diego Italian Food: A Culinary History of Little Italy and Beyond (History Press), Market Restaurant + Bar Cookbook: Seasonally Inspired Cuisine from Southern California (Globe Pequot Press), 100 Things To Do In San Diego Before You Die (Reedy Press), San Diego Food Finds Best Local Eats: 2017, 2018, 2019 (Maria Desiderata Montana), San Diego Food Finds Official Guidebook: 2020 (Maria Desiderata Montana), and The Inn at Rancho Santa Fe Cookbook. She is extensively published in several newspapers and magazines, where she has written a variety of food and entertainment stories as well as her own monthly recipe column. Maria has guest appeared on local radio and TV to share her knowledge of food and cooking, and regularly assists celebrity and high-profile chefs with cookbook projects.

Introduction

Aptly named "America's Finest City," San Diego is famous for a moderate climate, friendly attitude, health-conscious lifestyle, and endless natural and man-made attractions. It is the eighth-largest city in the United States and second-largest city in California. With nearly 16 million overnight visitors a year (another 15 million visits for a day trip), it's no wonder that tourism is the third largest industry in San Diego County, joining defense/military, international trade, and research (high-tech, communications, and biotech) as the main employers.

And it's not just a huge influx during the summer months, as statistics show only a moderate bump in tourism between June and September. People like to visit throughout the year, due to one of the mildest and predictable weather patterns in the country. It is one of the top five leisure vacation destinations in the US with nearly 90 percent of our visitors traveling for non-business reasons. The climate of San Diego is categorized as semi-arid or Mediterranean, with average high temperatures ranging from the mid-60s to upper-70s year-round. Measurable precipitation is recorded only around 40 total days every year, which is half to a third of the national average.

A recent study found that 86 percent of national chefs pointed to three hot tendencies in the culinary industry: locally sourced meats and seafood, locally grown produce, and sustainability. It is so true that diners want to know where their food is coming from and want to be sure it's nutritious for themselves and their families. San Diego's location makes it a perfect fit for this new direction, as fresh produce, seafood, and meats are easily sourced year-round. It is a true hotbed for the slow food movement, a progressive mind-set for preserving traditional and regional cuisines by incorporating local ingredients in a fashion that preserves the ecosystem. Basically, it is the antithesis of the fast-food epidemic. In this book, you will often see me mention menus that are driven by farm-to-table attitudes. And it is so true! Many of the restaurants regularly use produce from local farmers, and even their own on-site gardens, to complete their recipes. No pesticide or preservatives here. The seafood? It's usually locally caught, or harvested using a sustainable practice to ensure the environmental impact is minimal. The meats? Many local chefs will only choose farm-raised animals that are typically grass-fed and free of hormones. Not only is the food better tasting, it is more nutritious, and leaves you with a sense of goodwill toward the planet and people.

Since the city is located on the coast of the Pacific Ocean and immediately adjacent to the Mexican border, the cuisine has serious Hispanic and Asian influences. You'll see this trend throughout the book. California modern cuisine is a trend taking hold throughout the region, fusing several different cuisines and styles to make great dishes even more extraordinary. Asian fusion is really the same concept, only focusing on the many individual flavors and cooking styles of the orient, and melding them together on one menu and even in one dish. Of course, French and Mediterranean styles and flavors are also widely used to perfection. You will also notice other, lesser-seen cuisines becoming commonplace in almost every part of the city, including Indian, Latin American, African, and the Pacific Islands. Not to be outdone, there are plenty of traditional American restaurants, bakeries, dessertiers, and burger and pizza joints to satisfy any craving.

San Diego is an experience like no other. Obviously, it would be impossible to include every great restaurant within these pages, so the list has been narrowed to favorites. You are welcome to drop a note with your favorite destinations at sandiegofoodfinds.com. After all, food is meant for enjoyment and enrichment, and the choices are endless.

How to Use This Book

Altogether, San Diego contains more than 100 identified neighborhoods! In an effort to simplify your navigation, many of the adjacent neighborhoods are grouped into larger areas within the city. Each of the 13 areas has a dedicated chapter with restaurants listed in alphabetical order.

Price Code: The price range is covered in this book, immediately following the address listing, using the following guide.

$ Cheap: you can have a full meal for $10 or less here.

$$ Economical: $10 to $25 per person.

$$$ Moderate: $25 to $50 per person (a meal equivalent to an appetizer, entrée selection, and one alcoholic beverage).

$$$$ Expect to spend $50 to $75 for one appetizer, one entrée, and a glass or two of wine.

$$$$$ You will not walk out of this establishment having spent less than $75 to $100 per person; the sky's the limit.

Getting Around

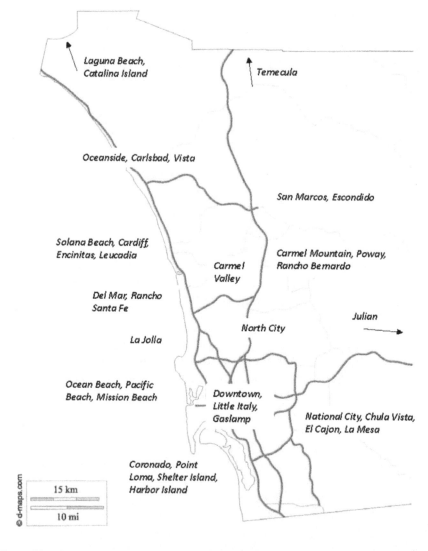

Laguna Beach, Catalina Island

Temecula

Oceanside, Carlsbad, Vista

San Marcos, Escondido

Solana Beach, Cardiff, Encinitas, Leucadia

Carmel Mountain, Poway, Rancho Bernardo

Carmel Valley

Del Mar, Rancho Santa Fe

Julian

North City

La Jolla

Ocean Beach, Pacific Beach, Mission Beach

Downtown, Little Italy, Gaslamp

National City, Chula Vista, El Cajon, La Mesa

Coronado, Point Loma, Shelter Island, Harbor Island

15 km

10 mi

© d-maps.com

Note: North City area includes the neighborhoods of Kearny Mesa, Mira Mesa, Clairemont, Old Town, Balboa, Mission Valley, Bankers Hill, Hillcrest, North Park, South Park and Kensington.

Walking

Depending on where you're at, this could be the most enjoyable option. Many of the areas in this book have central parts of town.

By Car

Renting a car during your visit is a very smart decision, unless you plan to remain in one area. It's best to plan far ahead, making sure you understand the city layout, and consider traffic patterns. One of the best resources of information is AAA (aaa.com). Fortunately, the roadways in this area are well designed to keep traffic flowing throughout the county. However, rush-hour traffic is as regular as the weather, so you should account for this added congestion between 7:30 to 9 a.m. and 4 to 6 p.m. Carpools are given a break on the main highways, and only require 2 or more passengers in the car. There is ample parking available in pay lots, along the streets (bring change for the meters between 8 a.m. and 5 p.m.), and in centrally located parking garages.

The main freeways in San Diego County are I-5 (runs north/ south along the coast from the US–Mexico border through Oceanside), I-805 (runs north/south parallel to I-5, stretching inland from south of Del Mar to Downtown), I-15 (runs north/south through the inland area, from South County through Escondido and into Temecula), and I-8 (runs east/west from the East County to Ocean Beach). There are dozens of other smaller highways and thoroughfares throughout the county, including the famous 101, running from La Jolla to Oceanside, with stunning views of the coastline, and plenty of stoplights along the way.

By Rideshare Services or Taxi

Being a car-centric city, San Diego is certainly not similar to the taxi havens of Los Angeles, New York, or Chicago. For those car-less individuals with interest in getting from Point A to Point B most efficiently, there are a number of convenient options. Although traditional taxis were the norm not many years ago, new app friendly ride sharing services have become the standard. Uber and Lyft are the most popular examples, where you are able to hail, monitor and pay for your ride without shelling out cash. These services also offer the advantage of rapid availability, as riders seldom wait longer than 10 minutes from any destination in the county. If you're in the downtown core or airport, you can also call a taxi, as these are the busiest locations requiring transportation. A number of websites can help you locate a good taxi service and also provide an estimated fare, including taxifarefinder.com or taxiwiz.com. For a more pampered experience, consider private town car or limo. There are plenty of options available online, and it is a booming business for the affluent in southern California.

By Bus, Trolley, and Train

The San Diego Metro and North County Transit systems (sdcommute.com) maintain one of the best options for travelers that want to see various areas without the hassle of a car rental. This includes an extensive light rail/trolley system that services 53 stations, nearly 90 fixed bus routes, and 2 commuter rail lines. The trolley covers a lot of ground, from the US–Mexican border, throughout downtown, up to Little Italy and the popular Old Town, and east through La Mesa, El Cajon, and Santee. Stops along the way include Petco Park (home of the San Diego Padres) and Qualcomm Stadium for other large sporting events. The Coaster is a commuter train that runs along the coast from Oceanside to downtown and teams up with its sister, the Sprinter, which runs inland from Oceanside to Escondido. The services also link into the Amtrak Pacific Surfliner and Orange County Metrolink. Fares vary depending on the length of your trip, but it's a scenic and convenient way to cover a lot of ground during your visit.

By Ferry

No visit to America's Finest City would be complete without taking a ride on the ferry across the scenic San Diego Bay. Enjoy the city skyline, views of the naval base and majestic ships, and of course the famous Coronado Bridge, stretching over 2 miles and 200 feet high over the Bay between downtown and Coronado Island. The Coronado Commuter Ferry (sdhe.com/san-diego-commuter-ferry.html) takes morning and afternoon commuters across San Diego Bay from the San Diego Broadway Pier, to the Naval Air Station North Island, and the Coronado Ferry Landing. San Diego Harbor Excursion (sdhe.com/ san-diego-bay-ferry.html) operates ferry shuttles directly to and from the San Diego Broadway Pier, the Coronado Ferry Landing, and the Fifth Avenue Landing. Prices start at $5.00 each way (children under 3 are free). You also have many choices of day and dinner cruises throughout the year, where you can enjoy the skyline and water activities while sipping champagne or dancing the night away.

Oceanside, Carlsbad & Vista

This coastal tri-city area is on the far north edge of San Diego County and just south of Camp Pendleton, one of the busiest Marine Corp bases in the US. There is a very strong military presence and community support for the local troops, as seen in many of the local businesses. The expansive coastline is always busy with tourists and locals taking walks or just enjoying beach-style activities. Inland areas are dotted with commercial and residential communities in one of the larger sections of North County.

Oceanside is home to one of the longest wooden piers in the western United States. First built in 1888, this pier is central to the beach area and offers a 1,942-foot stroll of scenic beauty above the roaring Pacific. Perched at the end of the pier is Ruby's Diner, which is open every day and offers great American drive-in food, but without the cars! The nearby amphitheater is host to many musical and cultural events throughout the year. Approximately 1 mile north of the pier is Oceanside Marina, where you can join charter fishing and whale watching tours anytime of the year.

The inland part of the tri-city area is home to Vista, a city that operates 15 community parks—6 times the national average—that includes theaters, museums, recreation centers, picnic grounds, and athletic fields. Considered the "avocado capital of the world" in the 1940s and '50s, agriculture is still a strong component of this area.

This area also has a strong business focus, with over 800 companies calling Vista home. Be sure to visit the Antique Gas & Steam Engine Museum, with a collection focused on the period from 1849–1950. Unique from many museums, the equipment is maintained in operating condition and used for demonstrations.

©*Maria Desiderata Montana*

333 Pacific, 333 N. Pacific St., Oceanside, CA 92054; (760) 433-3333; 333pacific.com; California Modern; $$$. Located near the historic Oceanside pier, this gorgeous restaurant features indoor and outdoor dining areas; lively music, a big-screen TV, and an electrifying bar and lounge. The inside dining room offers a very nice ocean view, but the large outdoor patio gives you a closer view of the Pacific. If you are a vodka connoisseur, this is the place for you. Choose from 100-plus vodkas from around the world while indulging in California-centric seafood, sushi, signature steaks, and chops. Steaks are prepared in an 1,800°F broiler, ensuring a tender and juicy center with a perfectly charred outer crust. You can't go wrong with the 333 Filet Trio Medallions cooked oscar style with crab and asparagus, bleu cheese crusted with bacon-tomato jam, brandied peppercorn cream, and fried onions. Don't want a steak? Venture out and try the Steamed Carlsbad Mussels, or the Escargot with bleu cheese fondue.

Barrel Republic, 215 N Coast Hwy. Oceanside, CA 92054; (760) 435-0042; barrelrepublic.com; Gastropub; $$. Barrel Republic boasts a modern yet rustic barn atmosphere complete with wood barrels filled with 60 tap handles for beer aficionados to freely pour and enjoy. Whenever possible, seasonal, organic, and local ingredients are uniquely created for the Barrel; scratch, fresh and original craft food for craft beer. Our favorites include Bacon Wrapped Pork Belly, Smoked Salmon and Lamb Meatballs, Charcuterie Board with Angel's Salumi, House-Made Soba Noodle Salad, and of course the Barrel Burger. The kitchen chef and staff, together with other restaurants in Oceanside, are on a pilot program to become totally zero waste, returning melon skins, lettuce cores, etc., back to the farm for composting. Recycling every possible product is the goal. This is in conjunction with the City of Oceanside. Multiple locations can be found throughout San Diego.

Campfire, 2725 State Street, Carlsbad, CA 92008; (760) 637-5121; thisiscampfire.com; American; $$$. This north county restaurant offers a vast modernist edge indoor/outdoor space with a 25-seat copper bar that invites guests to enjoy a market-driven menu paired with classic cocktails. Enjoy an interesting take on dining through ancient and primitive live-fire cooking techniques. In the heart of the restaurant, a custom 12-foot hearth, powered by a Grillwork's grill, utilizes wood, charcoal, embers and ash to lend hints of smoke to locally sourced and sustainable meats and seafood. Highlights of the menu include the Leg of Lamb and S'mores for dessert.

Casa de Bandini, 1901 Calle Barcelona, Carlsbad, CA 92009; (760) 634-3443; casadebandini.com; Mexican; $$$. Located in the Forum Shopping Center in Carlsbad, this beautiful restaurant owned by Diane Powers features a wide array of authentic and regional Mexican entrees. The atmosphere is as festive as it gets with colorful Mexican decorations and strolling mariachis stopping by your table. An outdoor patio decked out with colorful lights and umbrellas is a hip gathering place in the evenings, so grab a seat when you can. Watch a seniorita make tortillas by hand, while your server brings you a giant margarita from the cantina featuring over 50 of the most popular tequilas. My favorite is the specialty Jalapeno cocktail with Tanteo Jalapeno Tequila, triple sec, agave, fresh lime juice and cilantro. Great food choices are the traditional Huevos Rancheros Mexicanos, the Shredded Beef Chimichanga, the Enchiladas Verdes filled with cheese, or the Fish Tacos de Bandini served with black beans and arroz amarillo, with salsa fresca on the side. Healthy dining options include fresh salads, vegetarian items, and a variety of gluten-free choices. Other restaurants by Diane Powers include Casa de Pico in La Mesa, Casa Guadalajara in Old Town, and Casa Sol y Mar in the Del Mar Highlands Town Center.

Don's Country Kitchen, 2885 Roosevelt St., Carlsbad, CA 92008; (760) 729-2274; donscountrykitchen.com; American; $$. Reminiscent of a country inn with floral tablecloths and lacy ivory valences bordering the windows, this cute little eatery offers a ton of made-from-scratch specialties for breakfast and lunch. There are about six tables inside, as well as a long counter with barstools, and a small outdoor patio. Breakfast is a filling feast, with hearty helpings of fluffy homemade Buttermilk Biscuits topped with their famous country sausage gravy, or a luscious Banana Pecan Waffle Nut topped with whipped cream. For lunch, warm your soul with one of their hearty soups, especially the clam chowder, split pea, or chicken tortilla. Other influential dishes include the house roasted Hot Turkey Sandwich, topped with turkey gravy, and served with mashed potatoes, Don's made from scratch country chili, or the Beer Battered Fish and Chips. With reasonable prices and fast and friendly service, you can't go wrong here. Additional location is at 1938 S. Coast Hwy, Oceanside, CA 92054.

Flying Pig Pub & Kitchen, 626 S. Tremont St., Oceanside, CA 92054; (760) 453-2940; flyingpig.pub; American; $$$. Located on a rather quiet residential street just 1 block west from the South Coast Highway, this small gastropub is a hidden gem. Husband-and-wife team Rodney and Aaron Browning have deep experience in the local culinary community, working with some of the most respected chefs in Southern California. This eatery is dedicated to the slow-food movement, a farm-to-table philosophy utilizing locally sourced and fresh ingredients. Rustic American cuisine is featured throughout the menu, with a touch of Southern-style comfort. Favorite menu items include the Jidori Farms Airline Chicken

Breast or the Compart Duroc Pork Cutlet. And if you leave without having the Fried Calamari with garlic aioli, you've really missed out. They offer a collection of craft beers on tap and in bottles, as well as a great selection of wines by the bottle or glass. Local artists are featured on a dedicated wall and available for purchase. Reservations are recommended on the weekend, as this cozy hangout is popular with the locals for its high-quality offerings. Additional location is at 230 S. Santa Fe Ave, Vista, CA 92084.

Gregorio's, 300 Carlsbad Village Dr., Carlsbad, CA 92008; (760) 720-1132 gregoriosrestaurant.com; Italian; $$$. Reminiscent of a big Italian kitchen, the service at Gregorio's is friendly, the atmosphere is warm and welcoming, and the food is reasonably priced. Order a specialty pizza while catching a game on the TV indoors or on the enclosed heated patio, which has a partially enclosed awning and two more TVs. Bring the family because there is a little something on the menu for everyone, including appetizers and salads as well as specialty sandwiches, pizza, pasta, chicken, steak, and seafood. Try the Seasonal Fresh Catch of the Day served Sicilian style with a mushroom risotto. Some like it hot, and the Shrimp Fra Diavlo (Spicy Marinara and Linguini) fits the bill. Don't despair: you can cool off your tongue with a velvety rich spumoni-flavored gelato afterward!

Harney Sushi, 301 Mission Ave., Oceanside, CA 92054; (760) 967-1820; harneysushi.com; Asian Fusion; $$$. Harney Sushi, located near the Oceanside pier, is sexy-chic and sophistication all rolled into one. Accented with the color red, this roomy restaurant can seat up to 150 people inside. Grab a seat in one of the black booths, or at the environmentally friendly sushi and sake bars made of concrete and recycled glass. Of course, there is always room on the spacious outdoor patio if you prefer. No matter where you are in this restaurant, you'll be tapping your chopsticks to the beat of DJ music while indulging on elaborate seafood concoctions that melt in your mouth. My favorite rolls are the Bomb James Bomb and the Flaming Lip. On a mission to protect the health of our oceans and bodies, sushi creations from a sustainable seafood menu are constantly reinvented here, keeping guests wondering what flavor combination will come next. Additional location is at 3964 Harney St, San Diego, CA 92110.

Jalisco Cantina, 213 N Coast Highway, Oceanside CA 92054; (760) 429-1679; thejaliscocantina.com; Mexican; $$. Oceanside's iconic Coast Highway is home to hot and spicy Jalisco Cantina. Their name, "Jalisco," combines two Nahuatl words and is the language of the Aztecs meaning "sandy place." It is also home to the blue agave plant and some of the finest tequilas in the world. Jalisco Cantina's scratch kitchen dishes out some authentic Central-Coastal Mexican specialties that raise the bar on fresh Mex, and are developed to pair beautifully with their line-up of fine tequilas and uniquely prepared hand-crafted cocktails. Five fresh taco selections are offered, and cocktails are off the charts with both tequila and mescal flights being offered along with specialty margaritas.

Jeune et Jolie, 2659 State St, Carlsbad, CA 92008; (760) 637-5266; jeune-jolie.com; French; $$. Carlsbad's new-wave French restaurant whose name translates to "young and beautiful," was named one of Esquire's Best New Restaurants, class of 2019, drawing national attention to the burgeoning restaurant scene in North County San Diego. Jeune et Jolie offers diners a globally-inspired French menu, exploratory cocktails, and impeccable interiors designed by Bells and Whistles. Jeune et Jolie has established itself as a vital force in the reimagining of State Street, along with its sister restaurant Campfire, a mere two blocks south, which received Bib-Gourmand status from the California Michelin Guide.

KoKo Beach Restaurant, 2858 Carlsbad Blvd., Carlsbad, CA 92008; (760) 434-6868; kokobeach.com; American; $$$. Specialty of the house prime rib, hand-cut steaks, and fresh seafood have kept the locals coming for years to this cozy, old-fashioned hideaway with a dark atmosphere and red-leather booths. Enjoy breakfast or lunch, and don't worry about dinner, because they are open daily until midnight. Entree prices are reasonable and include a choice of soup or dinner salad, steak fries, baked potato, house rice, or fresh vegetables. Try the Roasted Prime Rib, the 1-full-pound sweet red Alaskan king crab legs served with drawn butter and lemon, or the slow-cooked barbecue baby back ribs finished on the char broiler. A cozy bar and lounge with a fireplace is the perfect setting for an after-dinner nightcap.

Masters Kitchen and Cocktail 208 S Coast Hwy, Oceanside, CA 92054; (760) 231-6278; mastersoceanside.com; American; $$. Located just blocks from the beach in the heart of Oceanside, Masters Kitchen and Cocktail offers fresh, local and artisan food served in a warm and inviting atmosphere. Situated in an industrial space that was once a well-remembered drag car shop, this restaurant keeps its authentic character, offering a separate bar with communal seating for guests to sip on traditional craft cocktails.

Park 101, 3040 Carlsbad Blvd, Carlsbad, CA 92008; (760) 434-2217; park101carlsbad.com; American; $$. Park 101 is an 8,000-square foot multi-use and plaza-style community dining and lounging area in the heart of Carlsbad Village. Think fried pickles and beer for the adults, and cotton candy for the kids. Enjoy lip-smacking BBQ ribs and brisket, plus regional wines and bites offered on the upper Tamarack View Deck with cozy fire pits. On the ground level, guests can enjoy fresh juices, sandwiches, espresso, ice cream sandwiches, handmade donuts, and more!

Ruby's Diner, 5630 Paseo Del Norte, Carlsbad, CA 92008; (760) 931-7829; rubys.com; American; $$. Open since 1982, this 1940s-style diner is famous for its great food and spectacular service in a sparkling-clean restaurant. It's a nice walk along the Oceanside Pier, and Ruby's is located at the very end. Inside there are two levels, all with beautiful views of the Pacific. The view is as good as you would find in a higher end restaurant, but without the high prices. Imagine waterside dining and a hot and spicy burger topped with Sriracha Hot Chili Sauce, two slices of melted Pepper Jack cheese, jalapeños, thick-cut bacon, green leaf lettuce, tomato, cilantro, and Sriracha mayo. Add a sweet and savory Salted Caramel Shake with its delightful combination of rich caramel flavor, a hint of sea salt and creamy vanilla soft serve ice cream—could it get any better than that? Oh yes—Ruby's all-natural USDA Choice beef comes only from hormone- and antibiotic-free cattle, raised naturally and fed on pasture grass, natural grains, legumes, and corn, and then allowed to mature slowly for optimal flavor and tenderness. Look for additional Ruby's locations throughout San Diego.

Twenty/20 Grill and Wine Bar, 5480 Grand Pacific Dr., Carlsbad, CA 92008; (760) 827-2500; twenty20grill.com; California Modern; $$$. In a magnificent airy space at the Sheraton Carlsbad Resort & Spa, you will find this warm and inviting restaurant complete with an outdoor patio offering views of the Pacific Ocean and the ever-blooming Carlsbad Flower Fields. And since the hotel is adjacent to LEGOLAND, you might see worn-out parents hunched over the bar unwinding over a much-needed martini. A diverse and globally inspired menu leans on playful flavor combinations from locally grown fresh ingredients for breakfast, lunch, and dinner. Choose from a nice selection of affordable wines, draught beers, and specialty cocktails.

Vivace, 7100 Aviara Resort Dr., Carlsbad, CA 92011; (760) 448-1234; vivace-restaurant.com; Italian; $$$$. Italian for "alive," Vivace at Park Hyatt Aviara provides an elegant yet sophisticated ambiance with an irresistible contemporary Italian menu. A warm fireplace keeps diners warm and cozy in the winter months, and dining alfresco on the terrace is the perfect option for summer. The pastas are made in-house daily, including a mouth-watering Rigatoni with Braised Short rib Bolognese. Pick a great wine from Italy off the wine list, and your dinner is complete.

WR Kitchen & Bar (by Wood Ranch), 2668 Gateway Rd Suite 170, Carlsbad, CA 92009; (442) 232-4440; wrkitchenbar.com; New American; $$. As the offshoot of the Southern California-based barbecue chain in Laguna Niguel (Wood Ranch), WR Kitchen & Bar in Carlsbad brings fast-casual flair to barbecue and comfort food lovers. Housed at The Square at Bressi Ranch, this 3,900 square-foot barbecue haven is tailored to today's more sophisticated, time-challenged guest. Think delicious, high quality food in a casually-upscale environment. Featuring a wood-fired open kitchen, guests can choose from an a la carte menu, allowing for more customizable options in selection and portion size. The eatery has also honed its menu to cater to a wider price range, with items to accommodate everyone's budget. WR Kitchen & Bar features Wood Ranch favorites, including Tri Tip, Baby Back Ribs, BBQ Chopped Salad, and house-made desserts. Don't miss the tacos filled with your choice of brisket, pulled pork, salmon roasted chicken, tri tip or roasted cauliflower. Additional crowd-pleasers from the eatery's original locations include Crispy Buffalo Cauliflower and Wood-Grilled Shishito Peppers. A full bar includes hand-crafted batch cocktails, craft beers on draft, and several outstanding value-priced wines.

Wrench and Rodent Seabasstropub, 1815 South Coast Highway, Oceanside, CA 92054; (760) 271-0531;seabasstropub.com; Sushi; $$$. Considered one of the most innovative sushi restaurants in North County, their approach is unconventional, resulting in complex flavors that keep patrons coming from all parts of Southern California. On any given day, both the indoor dining room and outdoor patio are packed with guests enjoying a different kind of Japanese-inspired cuisine. Menu items are created from only the freshest ingredients brought in daily by local purveyors. Don't be surprised if the fish enjoyed on your plate was caught less than 24 hours prior, and much of the produce is from farms located a short driving distance away. But what is most

Solana Beach, Cardiff-by-the-Sea, Encinitas & Leucadia

Located between Carlsbad to the north and Del Mar to the south, these oceanfront communities are stunningly scenic yet extremely laid-back. Dotted with vintage bungalows and quaint eateries, this is a local hot spot for the surfer and foodie alike. Nothing says vintage California more than this quaint area of San Diego. Although mostly centered on the historic Highway 101, these areas also stretch inland, where newer communities have developed.

Solana Beach is the southernmost community, where every residence and business are only a short distance to the ocean. Eden Gardens is one of the oldest residential areas of Solana Beach, formed in the 1920s by Mexican farmers. Some of the finest Mexican restaurants in San Diego are still operating here. One block east of Highway 101 is the Cedros District, which has grown into an upscale design district that attracts many artisans, decorators, and antiques dealers. Just a little farther north is Cardiff-by-the-Sea, formed in 1911 and named after the founders' birthplace of Cardiff, Wales. Many of the major streets in this community also bear familiar names from the UK. The town is very small, so most residents have views of the ocean and can easily walk between the ocean, community parks, and business areas. A must-see is the number of restaurants located directly on the beach in an area dubbed "Restaurant Row." Cardiff also includes the 900-acre San Elijo Lagoon Ecological Reserve, which is the largest coastal wetland in San Diego County and home to nearly 300 different bird species throughout the year.

Still farther north is Encinitas. The downtown area along Highway 101 is a 100-year-old coastal shopping district with examples of historic architecture, quaint shops, sidewalk cafes, and restaurants highlighted by beautiful flower baskets lining the street. Many residents consider Encinitas the Flower Growing Capital, and the city has been strategically developed around the preexisting flower growers. Be sure to visit the San Diego Botanic Gardens, which includes 4 miles of garden trails, flowering trees, majestic palms, and the nation's largest bamboo collection. Located directly on a cliff top off Highway 101 is the Self Realization Center. Founded in 1920 as a focal point for yoga and well-being, it is situated overlooking the ocean in a serene garden-like setting, and is open to the public. Also included in Encinitas is one of the most famous surfing locations on the Pacific, Swami's Beach, which is located at the far south end of town. The steakhouse genre is alive, well and thriving in Encinitas.

Last but not least is Leucadia, a small area just north of Encinitas, right along Highway 101. Many residents consider it a sub-town of Encinitas. Beaches here are difficult to find and not frequented by tourists, as the only access from the sheer cliffs are a few well-designed stairways leading to the rocky shore. These are very popular with the local surfing community

©Maria Desiderata Montana

101 Diner, 552 S. Coast Hwy. 101, Encinitas, CA 92024; (760) 753- 2123; American; $$. This roadside hole-in-the-wall/meets greasy spoon/meets diner is packed with locals who wouldn't dream of going anywhere else for breakfast and lunch. When you walk in, the friendly wait staff will greet you with a smile and treat you like you've been coming in for years. In fact, they'll most likely remember you by name. Have a seat in one of the vintage booths and you'll be transported into a vintage beach-town hangout. If you've never had fresh-cut pork chops and eggs for breakfast, try it here, including your choice of potato and bread. The spicy beef Louisiana sausage or corned beef hash will knock your socks off. Warm and like nothing else you've ever tasted, don't miss the fluffy pineapple or banana nut pancakes. You'll love this place!

Alfonso's of La Jolla, 437 South Highway 101 #301, Solana Beach, CA 92075; (858) 454-2232; alfonsoslj.com, Mexican; $$. Experience fine Mexican dining at Alfonso's where family recipes have been handed down from generation to generation. Specialties include Carne Asada and Puerto Nuevo style lobster tail.

A Little Moore Coffee Shop, 1030 North Highway 101, Leucadia, CA 92024; (760) 753-8228; American; $$. Start your morning off right with a full-size breakfast at this vintage roadside diner, complete with French Country white windows, old-style tables, and a shiny countertop bar where you can sit and observe your eggs sizzling on an open griddle. Unlike the many chain coffee shops in town, this cute little cafe will take you back to the simpler life of the 1950s. That's when this little gem was first established in the quieter area of Highway 101 north of Encinitas. The locals know they can count on friendly, fast service and affordable prices while they get their fill of omelets, pancakes, and French toast. Do you like steak and eggs? They have it, along with Polish sausage or teriyaki chicken and eggs. Other substantial good-morning eats include a chili cheese omelet and eggs Benedict. And of course, you have to try their coffee! Also open for lunch.

Bangkok Bay, 731 South Highway 101, 1B1, Solana Beach, CA 92075; (858) 792-2427; bangkok-bay.com; Thai; $$$. You'll fall in love with the dimly lit ambiance and the Thai decor and foliage. This hidden gem nestled in the Mercado Del Sol complex reflects a rich variety of northeastern Thai drinks, crepes, soups, salads, noodles, curries, and desserts. Go with a bunch of friends and share a variety of entrees around the table. Try the half honey roasted duck on top of a bed of steamed young spinach, broccoli, and carrots topped with a honey sauce; kua rice noodles stir-fried with egg, brown sauce, and bean sprouts, then sprinkled with scallions and crushed peanuts; and of course, the fried bananas with coconut ice cream for dessert.

Beach Grass Cafe, 159 South Highway 101, Solana Beach, CA 92075; (858) 509-0632; beachgrasscafe.com; Organic/Health Food; $$. You can dress up or come in flip-flops to this novel cafe with its white tablecloths in an informal setting. Guests who walk through these doors can expect a fabulous meal with friendly and personal service, and there are plenty of vegetarian options. Try the Sweet Corn Polenta roasted in a banana leaf with two eggs and spicy Louisiana sausage. Another great breakfast item that's on the sweeter side and very popular with the locals is the luscious Maple, Bacon and Cheddar Pancakes paired with a dark roast coffee. For lunch don't miss the Chicken Tropical Salad or the Grilled Steak Kahlua Pork Tacos.

Blue Ribbon Artisan Pizzeria, 897 South Coast Highway, 101, #102, Encinitas, CA, 92024; (760) 634-7671; blueribbonpizzeria.com; Pizza; $$. Even with the long waits for dinner, this charming neighborhood pizza joint does pizza the organic, sustainable, and local way. The pizza dough undergoes a three-day fermentation process, mozzarella cheese is stretched by hand daily, and the fennel sausage is made from sustainable Berkshire pork on-site. Delicious pizzas are topped with unique ingredient combinations and cooked in a wood-burning oven. Favorites include truffled four-cheese pizza with mozzarella, bleu cheese, Parmigiana Reggiano, ricotta, and chives or the pizzaiolo topped with the chef's seasonal selections. As for drink options, Diet Coke isn't an option at this au naturel establishment. You will, however, find plenty of local craft beers on tap as well as organic, sustainable, and biodynamic wines.

Breakfast Republic, 251 N. El Camino Real, Encinitas, CA 92024; (760) 452-2121; breakfastrepublic.com; American; $$. This eclectic eatery in Encinitas boasts a colorful décor with humorous signage that instantly puts you in a good mood. Owner and restaurateur Johan Engman, who wanted to hone in on one thing and do it right, inspired Breakfast Republic's egg-ceptional concept and menu. Not to mention the meal he loves most is breakfast. At 3,500 square feet plus an additional 700 square foot patio space, there is also an 'egg-cellent' lounge area with egg chairs and tables. Some of our favorite nostalgia-inspired dishes served with a twist include Oreo Cookie Pancakes, Pineapple Upside Down Pancakes, Lemon and Coconut French Toast, and Mushroom and Pesto Benedict with Button and Oyster Mushrooms, Red Peppers, Spinach, Hollandaise & Pesto Sauce. Multiple locations can be found throughout San Diego.

Chief's Burgers and Brew, 124 Lomas Santa Fe Drive, Suite 108, Solana Beach, CA 92075; (858) 755-2599; chiefsburgers.com; Burgers; $$. Sports fans pack local sports bars on weekends to watch their favorite games, and this place is no exception. But beware: The owners and regulars are die-hard Denver Bronco fans, so the bar on NFL Sundays is filled with orange jerseys and screaming fans. It's all in good fun and competition, so feel free to wear your favorite team with pride and join the party. With great burgers, 23 TVs, lots of windows, and an outdoor patio, you will be cheering with new friends in no time. All burgers are prepared with ½-pound Angus beef except for the massive Super Chief One Pound Burger consisting of two patties with double cheese, lettuce, tomato, onion, and Thousand Island dressing. From fried dill pickle sticks to jalapeño poppers, and a heading on the menu called "Everything but the Kitchen Sink," everyone in your party will find something they like to eat!

Chuao Chocolatier, 2350 Camino Vida Roble, Suite 101, Carlsbad, CA 92011; (760) 476-0197; chuaochocolatier.com; Chocolate; $$. If you aren't a chocolate lover now, you might become one after a visit to this one-of-a-kind artisan chocolate shop. Named after a legendary cacao-producing region of central Venezuela, Chuao was founded in Encinitas in 2002 by Venezuelan-born brothers Michael and Richard Antonorsi. You will be chew-wowed with a sensual and spicy experience from these handcrafted world-class chocolates made with all-natural ingredients. Crazy and crafty flavor combinations include dark chocolate caramel fudge "Firecracker" with chipotle chile, salt, and popping candy, the "Chevere" with goat cheese, Pear Williams, and crushed black pepper butter cream, and the Cinco de Mayo with lemon tequila dark chocolate ganache topped with a preserved lemon chip.

Cicciotti's Trattoria Italiana & Seafood, 1933 San Elijo Ave., Cardiff-by-the-Sea, CA, 92007; (760) 634-2335; cicciottis.com; Italian; $$$. Chef, restaurateur, and author Gaetano Cicciotti likes to cook his classic northern and southern Italian family recipes at this eatery just a step from the Cardiff beach. There is plenty of seating at the windows looking out over the Pacific, and also a spacious bar area. Lunch is a good time to visit if you like it less crowded. Choose the spaghetti and homemade meatballs or the in-house ravioli stuffed with fresh ricotta cheese and spinach, sautéed in a fresh tomato sauce and served with house salad or soup. Friday and Saturday are busy with live entertainment and a fun Italian wait staff. You'll have no problem finding a great label from the wine list while you wait for the stuffed pizza with mozzarella, gorgonzola cheese, and walnuts—there's nothing like it! Additional location is at 595 Grand Ave, Carlsbad, CA 92008.

Claire's on Cedros, 246 North Cedros Avenue, Solana Beach, CA 92075; (858) 259-8597; clairesoncedros.com; Organic/Health Food; $$. With a sustainable building and menu, this is the first LEED (Leadership in Energy and Environmental Design) Platinum–certified restaurant in San Diego. The menu is seasonal, but you will always find the award-winning original cinnamon or multigrain Clairecakes. Your morning sugar fix comes from the utterly decadent Bananas Foster French Toast stuffed with homemade ricotta cheese, topped with toasted pecans and fresh bananas, all served with a side of rum infused maple syrup. Egg lovers will savor a variety of hearty and healthful omelets and specialty items including Tuscan Benedict with homemade hollandaise and a delicious Short Rib Hash. Decorated like a country cottage, choose to sit in the warm and inviting dining room, or on the outdoor patio next to a bubbling fountain.

Crush, 437 S. Hwy. 101, #112, Solana Beach, CA 92075; (858) 481-CRUSH (2787); solanabeachcrush.com; Italian; $$$. This neighborhood Italian eatery is a favorite among the locals for its modish design, authentic Italian cuisine, and late-night happy hour scene. Enjoy a classically modern Italian menu featuring local and organic ingredients paired with over 160 bottles of hand-selected International wines. Live music is offered throughout the week, and there's plenty of seating on comfortable couches or outside next to the tabletop fire pit. Happy hour is especially busy. The restaurant is an extension of its sister restaurant of the same name, which has been delighting diners in Chico, California, for several years. This beautiful coastal destination offers lunch and dinner—with standout dishes including Eggplant Parmigiana, Fettuccine ale Vongole, and Cioppino. Now that's my kind of Italian!

Death by Tequila, 569 S Coast Hwy 101, Encinitas, CA 92024; (760) 782-2240; deathbytequila.com; Latin American; $$. Enjoy a menu that draws inspiration from the farm and local ingredients, while a simple and clean décor compliments the beautifully presented cocktails and cuisine. An eye-catching multi-layer and hand-painted Baja inspired mural by a local artist covers an entire wall, showcasing the surf cultures of Baja Mexico and Encinitas. The tequila program is curated with the intention of finding unique tequilas and mezcals that are high-quality, but also have a unique story.

East Coast Pizza, 2015 San Elijo Ave., Cardiff-by-the-Sea, CA 92007; (760) 944-1599; ecp-sd.com; Pizza; $. No doughy, soggy pizza crust here. East Coast serves the closest thing to the Big Apple in these parts. Pizzas are cooked in a brick oven with a good variety of traditional selections (meat lovers with meatballs, sausage, and pepperoni) and more contemporary options like the artichoke special, spicy chicken, homemade pesto, and Hawaiian barbecue with chicken and pineapple.

Fidel's Little Mexico, 607 Valley Ave., Solana Beach, CA 92075; (858) 755-5292; fidelslittlemexico.com; Mexican; $$. Imagine walking into a neighborhood barbershop in the 1960s and having Owner Fidel Montanez cut your hair and offer you a taco for lunch. Seems the tacos became even more popular than the haircuts, so Montanez turned the place into a neighborhood cantina for the locals to hang out in. When the locals spread the word about the authentic food, the place boomed with business, and Montanez converted his two-story residence into three different levels and named the place Fidel's. This festive place is always packed. Favorite food choices include the meatball soup, a massive shredded beef burrito, and chile relleno filled with Monterey Jack cheese.

Green Acre Campus Pointe, 10300 Campus Point Dr, San Diego, CA 92121, (858) 450-9907, greenacresd.com; New American; $$. Celebrated Chef Brian Malarkey and team commemorate seasonal farm to table organic ingredients at this chic and rustic eatery. Diners come here for the comfortable and relaxed atmosphere, expansive outdoor patios, and on site organic gardens. There is also a counter-service Café located at 3535 General Atomics Court.

Ki's Restaurant, 2591 South Coast Highway 101, Cardiff-by-the-Sea, CA 92007; (760) 436-5236; kisrestaurant.com; Organic/Health Food; $$$. This is one of Cardiff's best-kept secrets. Located just across the street from the Cardiff State Beach, Ki's offers a full spectrum of natural and organically raised foods without additives and preservatives. Choose from a fine selection of organic juices, smoothies, omelets, pancakes, salads, wraps, seafood, and meats. For breakfast try the tofu scramble in tamari spices and olive oil, and for lunch it's the thick millet veggie burger baked golden brown with cheese. If you visit for dinner, try the butternut squash soft rolled tacos. Gluten-free and vegan options are also available.

Lotus Cafe & Juice Bar, 765 S. Coast Hwy. 101, Encinitas, CA 92024; (760) 479-1977; lotuscafeandjuicebar.com; Organic/Health Food; $$. The Lumberyard in Encinitas is home to many trendy restaurants, and this is one of them. With indoor and outdoor seating for about 100 people, this healthy cafe is dedicated to serving fresh, locally sourced natural food at affordable prices. A comprehensive menu comprises many vegans, vegetarian, strict vegetarian and gluten-free options. Choose from savory and homemade organic soups, salads sandwiches, pasta, vegetarian entrees, fish and chicken entrees, kiddies' meals, fresh juices, smoothies, shakes, and desserts, even homemade vegan cupcakes. Such items as the Pipe's Whole Wheat Pita with falafel balls, hummus, and tahini-ginger sauce, and the Swami's Carrot shake with organic carrot juice, vanilla ice cream, cinnamon, and nutmeg make this place unusual.

Naked Cafe, 106 South Sierra Avenue, Solana Beach, CA 92075; (858) 259-7866; thenakedcafe.com; Organic/Health Food; $$. Want a "Plate of Prosperity" with organic quinoa for breakfast? Or how about a Goddess Wrap with sautéed sesame ginger tofu wrapped in a spinach tortilla for lunch? You'll find it here where wholesome foods are turned into healthy delights that the whole family can enjoy. The concept of this eatery is that eating foods "naked" in their simple, clean, and natural state will not only please your palate but also nurture your body and mind. Start the day with an organic espresso or an Asian coffee, and a Buff Breakfast Burrito with egg whites and grilled chicken. Other great choices include the Fuzzy Monkey Pancakes with roasted grains and fresh bananas or, for lunch, the ginger rice and black beans. Additional locations can be found in Encinitas, Carlsbad, and Point Loma.

Pacific Coast Grill, 2526 S. Coast Hwy 101, Cardiff, CA 92007; (760) 479-0721; pacificcoastgrill.com; American (New), $$$. If you're looking to dine just steps from the Pacific Ocean, then Pacific Coast Grill is the place for you. Two dining levels and a heated outdoor patio offer every guest an ocean view complete with magnificent sunsets. Order a craft cocktail and choose from a "Pacific Coast" cuisine that won't break the bank. Chilled appetizers are the draw here, especially the Seasonal Oysters on the Half Shell with passion fruit mignonette and cocktail sauces or the Ahi Poke Tower with Dungeness crab, spicy mayo, avocado, and crispy wonton chips. The Lobster and Shrimp Chowder with Applewood smoked bacon and oyster crackers should definitely be on your list, followed by the Coconut-Crab Crusted Mahi Mahi with vanilla jasmine rice, bok choy and apple cider-soy butter. The perfect ending to your meal is the Tahitian Coconut Cheesecake with passion fruit sauce and crispy coconut wafer.

Pamplemousse Grille, 514 Via de la Valle, Ste. 100, Solana Beach, CA 92075; (858) 792-9090; pgrille.com; French; $$$$. Since 1996, this comfortable, yet elegant restaurant located across from the Del Mar Race Track has been surprising guests with eclectic inspirations from Chef-Owner Jeffrey Strauss. Drawing from his childhood visits to his grandparents' New Jersey farm, as well as his many travels to Europe, Strauss offers guests a modish and upscale mix of French continental cuisine featuring grilled fish and meats. I recommend the crispy half duck with sautéed gnocchi and cherry balsamic reduction or the lamb stew with braised potato, green lentils, and a mélange of in-season baby vegetables. Don't miss spaghetti and meatballs every Sunday evening. As for the vino, educate yourself while making your selection from a 65-page book of local and international wines. Pamplemousse Grille has received many local and national awards including "Best Restaurant, People's Choice," San Diego Home & Gardens; "Best New Restaurant," "Best Caterer," and "San Diego's Best Chef," San Diego Magazine; and Zagat Rated #1 Restaurant in San Diego for three consecutive years.

Panera Bread, 667 San Rodolfo Dr., Solana Beach, CA 92075; (858) 481-0050; panerabread.com; Bakery; $$. "A loaf of bread in every arm" is Panera's motto. They truly believe that a great slice of bread is key to any meal. Yes, this is a chain, but it always provides a fresh, delicious lunch that will leave you satisfied throughout the day. Walking in through the big arched front entryway, you see a large counter in front of you filled with baskets of bread and pastries. As you stand in line, they almost always have a sample of their warm bread for you to nibble on while deciding what to order. Their Asiago Roast Beef sandwich includes tender shredded roast beef, lettuce, tomatoes, onions, cheddar cheese, horseradish sauce, and their crusty Asiago bread. All meals are served with a pickle slice and a choice of either their Panera brand chips, a piece of their French baguette bread, or an apple. Other talked-about items are their soups and salads, which value the finest ingredients within each season. Consider stopping by to grab a large sourdough loaf to serve with a meal you prepare at home. Multiple locations can be found throughout San Diego.

Parioli, 647 S. Hwy. 101, Solana Beach, CA 92075; (858) 755-2525; parioliitalianbistro.com; Italian; $$$. This wonderful Italian treasure is located in a simple little one-story beach house along Highway 101. This is the perfect place to enjoy upscale Mediterranean fare without the formality of a fine dining establishment. You'll be welcomed by a sunny front porch, prominent bar area, and stylish interior. The restaurant is co-owned and operated by two native Italian brothers whose food will draw you into another world. Chef Antonio admits there are many similarities between San Diego and southern Italy, and he utilizes seasonally fresh produce and ingredients in all his fabulous dishes. I fell in love with his Caprese salad, made with locally grown heirloom tomatoes, fresh mozzarella, and just the right touch of fresh basil, olive oil, and balsamic vinegar. For dinner, be sure to sample from the daily fish selections or one of the many traditional pasta dishes. Loyal patrons favor the homemade pappardelle or ravioli, prepared with the best available ingredients. The wine list is impressive, and there is also a large, interior courtyard area perfect for enjoying alfresco dining or reserving for a private party.

Pizza Port; 135 N Hwy 101, Solana Beach, CA 92075; 858) 481-7332; pizzaport.com; Pizza; $$. Want good pizza and great beer? This is the place! Pizza Port offered its first craft-brewed beers to patrons in 1992 and immediately gained popularity in San Diego's budding craft beer scene. Choose from a selection of menu items including salads, baked chicken wings, cheese sticks and more. Even build your own pizza on a traditional or whole grain beer crust! Multiple locations can be found throughout San Diego.

Q'ero, 564 S. Coast Hwy. 101, Encinitas, CA 92024; (760) 753-9050; qerorestaurant.com; Latin American; $$$. Every neighborhood needs a Latin American restaurant like this one. Peruvian and South American specialties influenced by ancient times and cultures are offered in a romantic and enchanting candlelit setting decorated with Peruvian-style artwork and tablecloths. Since this small and exclusive eatery is often booked for lunch and dinner, reservations are highly recommended. There are two seatings offered for dinner, and there is rarely an open table for walk-in customers, unless a cancellation has occurred. The signature Costillasen Jora is fork- tender beef short ribs braised in sacred Chicha de Jora- sacred corn beer, topped with house cured pickled vegetables, and served with a choice of kiwicha (amaranth) cake, mashed potatoes or sweet potato mash. Quinoa, an ancient grain once considered the gold of the Incas, makes for a beautiful salad when combined with seasonal apples, winter squash, and lacinato kale. Enjoy Peruvian and Brazilian beer and South American wine. Their second restaurant Casa del Q'ero is located at 815 Birmingham Dr, Cardiff, CA 92007.

Red Tracton's, 550 Via De La Valle, Solana Beach, CA 92075; (858) 755-6600; redtractonssteakhouse.com; Steak House; $$$$. Beef, it's what's for dinner at this classical restaurant that planted its roots in San Diego more than 25 years ago, although it was first established in 1948. If you're looking for one of the finest steak houses in town, this is the place. Begin your meal with their famous Green Goddess Salad, followed by a gigantic 24-ounce eastern prime rib and a colossal baked potato. Although the menu features a wide selection of meats and fish, there are also daily favorites, like home-style meat loaf and roasted turkey. A more "mature" crowd of regulars likes to frequent this restaurant, featuring live entertainment from the piano bar. The young people like the bar.

Samurai, 979 Lomas Santa Fe Dr., Solana Beach, CA 92075; (858) 481-0032; samuraijapaneserestaurant.com; Japanese; $$$. For 39 years, Samurai has been a mecca for Japanese food. From the cocktail bar to the multiple dining sections, including a sushi bar and large teppan grill, this place is fun for everyone. This is a more expensive restaurant that focuses on the quality of the food and drinks. The locals like to come in and dine on Monday and Tuesday evenings, which are slower nights. Weekends are louder, and there is more of a drinking crowd. The signature dish is definitely the chef's special specialty roll. I like sashimi, especially the tuna belly (toro) and the in-season live shrimp (amaebi). As for anti-sushi dishes, I highly recommend the chicken teriyaki and the assorted tempuras. If you decide you want red meat, invite your friends and dine around the teppan grill, which cooks the beef teriyaki or New York steak to a tender and juicy perfection.

St. Tropez Bakery & Bistro, 947 S. Coast Hwy. 101, No. 103-D, Encinitas, CA 92024; (760) 633-0084; sttbistro.com; Bakery; $$. Get your share of French bistro fare without the expensive plane ticket to France. Dine indoors or take a seat outside in the large outdoor patio, which resembles a sidewalk cafe—perfect for people watching with enough room for man's best friend. Walk by the large glass case inside, and take a long look at the traditional pastries. They also have a wide selection of filled cupcakes, cookies, patisseries, tarts, and cakes. If you're looking for a homemade treat on a special occasion, this is the place! I'm in love with the almond raspberry bars. Although my favorite time to visit is early in the morning for coffee and a light breakfast, the lunches and dinners are also excellent. Choose from soups, salads, hot and cold sandwiches, and plenty of delicious entrees. They also have a strong catering business throughout the local area. Multiple locations can be found throughout San Diego.

The Fish Market, 640 Via De La Valle, Solana Beach, CA 92075; (858) 755-2277; thefishmarket.com; Seafood; $$$. For over 30 years, this busy restaurant has been a Del Mar/Solana Beach favorite. Gather with friends at the popular oyster/cocktail bar and lounge. This is one of the few restaurants in town that serves a Crab Louie salad with traditional Thousand Island dressing. They also have delicious clam chowders available in traditional, New England, or Manhattan styles. A long list of fresh catches is available daily, cooked over mesquite wood broilers, and served with a choice of two side dishes. One of the most popular items on the menu is the hearty Dungeness Crab Cioppino, served with prawns, finfish, scallops, calamari, clams, mussels, cockles, and pasta with a house-made marinara sauce. Delicious! A retail fish market located at the front allows you to take home fresh, high-quality seafood selections, including the freshest fish, shellfish fish, smoked fish, and other menu items. There is an additional location is at 750 N. Harbor Dr, San Diego, CA 92101.

Tony's Jacal, 621 Valley Ave., Solana Beach, CA 92075; (858) 755-2274; tonysjacal.com; Mexican; $$. Opened in 1946 and tucked away in Solana Beach, Tony's Jacal is a casual joint that serves some of the most traditional Mexican food you will find in San Diego. Originally serving customers on weekends and only accommodating 26 guests at a time, this restaurant has really grown into the place to be for delicious authentic food. Because it is family owned, you really get a sense of home when eating here. The atmosphere is rustic, and when the mariachi band begins to play, you really get the full dining experience. Start your meal off with their spicy and flavorful salsa served with fresh tortilla chips, and order the classic margarita, which is served in a large glass—you'll be able to drink throughout the whole meal. Favorites include the chilies rellenos, carne asada tacos, and their classic tamales. Make sure to try the huevos rancheros, two eggs covered in tangy mild yellow and green chilies and topped with onions and tomatoes. Finish that off with the decedent Mexican hot chocolate and you are set for the day!

Trattoria Italiana, 530 N. Coast Hwy 101, Leucadia, CA 92024; (760) 634-2365; vigiluccis.com; Italian; $$$. With its largely Italian staff, diverse menu, and great wine list, it's no wonder this Encinitas eatery has become a favorite among regulars and Italians across the county who liken the fare to that served in Italy. One of their best appetizers is the non- fried, Luciana version of calamari, sautéed with garlic and white wine in a spicy marinara sauce. Come here for the large variety of fresh homemade pastas, especially the fettuccine with chicken in a classic Alfredo sauce. They also offer full-scale catering service with custom menus designed to meet the needs of small or very large occasions.

Union Kitchen and Tap, 1108 S. Coast Hwy. 101, Encinitas, CA 92024; (760) 230-2337; localunion101.com; American; $$$. Grab a barstool when you can, because this Encinitas hangout has become the talk of the town. Dinner is relaxing, yet somewhat elaborate, boasting artsy comfort food in a lively environment. Three separate dining areas welcome diners. The Oak Room is a bit more formal and subdued. The main bar area is casual, but fun, and the large roll-up garage doors allow for people watching outdoors. The Tap Room has seven TV's, perfect for viewing sports. Local craft beers and Southern-style girl drinks served in Mason jar glasses keep the locals happy. An upgraded menu includes local ingredients and Southern-style "lighter" fare cooked from scratch. Outrageous food surprises include Crawfish Popcorn with Cornmeal Crust, Farmhouse Meatballs, and Bourbon Braised Beef Cheeks. The star of the show is the Shrimp & Grits, a dish that takes 8 days to make and uses grits imported directly from the South. Additional location is at 333 Fifth Ave, San Diego, CA 92101.

VG's Donuts and Bakery, 106 Aberdeen Dr., Cardiff-by-the-Sea, CA 92007; (760) 753-2400; vgbakery.com; Bakery; $. There's really only one thing to say about this place, doughnuts! Made from scratch every day with no preservatives, these doughnuts are made with an old-fashioned style of baking that clearly tastes better. Open since 1969, they have been a favorite for generations of local residents as well as the surfing community who frequent the nearby beaches. Just stop by any morning and step in line. Although it can sometimes be quite long, it usually moves very quickly. Fortunately, doughnuts are baked twice daily, so there are always fresh selections available. Nearby businesses use them frequently for delivery to the hungry masses. They also carry a long list of special occasion and wedding cakes, cupcakes, pastries, muffins, cookies, breads, and bagels. During the holidays, they also feature a number of traditional and festive baked goods. But really, it's all about the maple or chocolate old- fashioned doughnut.

Carmel Valley, Del Mar & Rancho Santa Fe

New meets old in this area of San Diego, where historical and newly built residences share the land, sprawling from the Pacific Ocean to lushly landscaped communities spread inland for several miles. No visit to San Diego would be complete without visiting this haven for culinary excellence. Carmel Valley is one of the newest areas in San Diego, a sprawling, master-planned community that replaced acres of tomato fields over the past 2 decades. The restaurants in this area will be located in many of the town centers that dot the landscape to add convenience and a sense of community for the residents. Although the homes can be densely packed into distinct neighborhoods, Carmel Valley also retains open spaces, including the westernmost end of the San Dieguito River Park, a series of trails from the Pacific Ocean to the small town of Julian in the mountains. The nearby land is also used frequently by local hot air balloon companies as a take-off and landing area, especially in the summer, where you can often see colorful silhouettes in the afternoon sky, quietly floating over the vast valley with a stellar view of the Pacific.

The well-known city of Del Mar is located right on the coast and boasts some of the most expensive property near the Pacific. It also has a large concentration of the finest restaurants in the area, with nationally recognized chefs at the helm. If you're looking for a fine food experience, you'll never have to leave this small town. Summer is the most popular time to visit, as Del Mar is home to one of the largest fairs in North America based on attendance. June and July are filled with animal exhibits, contests, concerts, carnival attractions, and plenty of food. In August and September, you can join the flocks of spectators who try their luck at the Del Mar Racetrack, where Bing Crosby's crooning of "Where the Turf Meets the Surf" can still be heard before the first race every day.

Rancho Santa Fe is home to some of the most affluent residents in the continental US. The median property value is greater than $2.5 million. A small but centralized town center is dotted with high-end boutiques, galleries, and eateries. If you're looking to brush shoulders with the rich and famous, this is the place, at least in the few public areas. Most of the land is devoted to residential and agricultural use, with privacy getting a high priority. A strong equestrian presence is evident throughout the area at many exclusive horse parks and country clubs.

Rancho Santa Fe ©Maria Desiderata Montana

Addison at The Fairmont Grand Del Mar, 5300 Grand Del Mar Ct., San Diego, CA 92130; (858) 314-2000; addisondelmar.com; French; $$$$$. Timeless and classic, Addison within The Fairmont Grand Del Mar is the single most important destination for dining in San Diego. Relish in Relais & Chateaux Grand Chef William Bradley's artisanal approach to cooking, as well as enhance your culinary IQ. Contemporary French cuisine with an emphasis on seasonal California ingredients make for masterfully presented entrees with intense flavor characteristics. This is a destination to enjoy the true "dining experience," savored for hours over several courses, each a masterpiece in flavor and presentation. Watch as the formally clad attendants whisk your next course to the table, hesitating until everyone receives a covered dish, and then simultaneously lifting the lids to reveal the culinary art. Every aspect of the evening will leave an impression. Pair your meal with the perfect vino from Addison's world-class wine room. Menu highlights include avocado and golden caviar, Parmesan and arugula spring lamb, or the persillé with toasted pistachio purée, dates, and sauce chèvre. I would strongly suggest you choose one of the multicourse dinners, highlighting some of the best dishes in Bradley's repertoire, sequenced from savory to sweet, delighting your palate with every taste.

Americana, 1454 Camino Del Mar, Del Mar, CA 92014; (858) 794-6838; americanarestaurant.com; American; $$. This successful restaurant is nestled on a street corner in old Del Mar. Although they are open for breakfast, lunch, and dinner, it seems that folks like to gravitate here mostly for the morning fare, where you'll see people chatting and drinking cappuccinos while devouring buttermilk pancakes and eggs Benedict. Dine inside, or grab a chair at one of the cute tables along the front or to the side of the restaurant. While dining outside, passersby who can't help but get a glimpse of your food choice may want to join you. From green eggs and ham scrambled with spinach, pesto, and mozzarella to a homemade Belgian waffle, it's always busy for a reason. The locals know good food when they see it.

Amici's Ristobar, 5980 Village Way #B106, San Diego, CA 92130; (858) 847-2740; amicisristobar.com; Italian; $$. Located in the Village of Pacific Highlands Ranch just off Highway 56 and Carmel Valley Road, this trendy restaurant offers diners farm fresh California Italian cuisine in a sophisticated, yet comfortable setting. From Crispy Fried Baby Artichoke Hearts to Pasta with Braised Lamb or Fire Roasted Sea Scallops, made from scratch specialties are derivative of ingredients sourced locally or directly from Italy.

Board & Brew, 1212 Camino Del Mar, Del Mar, CA 92014; (858) 481 1021; boardandbrew.com; American; $. Established in 1979, this local legend is within walking distance of the Del Mar beach. Teenagers and surfer dudes of all ages like to hang out and eat some of the finest sandwiches in southern California. If you visit during lunch hours, expect a long, snaking line outside. Fortunately, the owners are well prepared for the onslaught, so everything moves quickly. Much of the available seating is on an outdoor patio, although many of the patrons are in grab-and-go mode. The most popular item is the Board Master, a roast beef and turkey breast combo with cheddar cheese and sweet-and-sour dressing served on a warm baguette. Also, a local favorite is the Turkado, with thick layers of turkey, Jack cheese, avocado, onion, tomato, and lettuce on sourdough bread. With generous portions and inexpensive prices to boot, this place is hard to beat! Multiple locations can be found throughout San Diego.

Caliente Mexican Food, 11815 Sorrento Valley Road, San Diego, CA 92121; (858) 259-9579; calientemexicanfood.com; Mexican; $. Popular among the locals, Caliente's is a great place to stop by for a quick bite. A menu of numerous dishes includes burritos, tacos, and combo plates at low prices. Whether you're a high school student from nearby West View High or Canyon Crest Academy, or just a businessman on his lunch break, Caliente's is a must try. Large portions are satisfying and I guarantee you won't leave hungry. The most popular item on the menu is the very large order of carne asada fries topped with carne asada steak, guacamole, sour cream, cheese, and salsa. Caliente's is also well known for its signature Caliente Burrito. This oversize burrito is perfectly compacted with a mixture of spices, salsa, shrimp, peas, and their house hot sauce, which is given on the side of every meal.

Chino Farm, 6123 Calzada del Bosque, Rancho Santa Fe, CA 92067 (off Via de la Valle, S6); Recorded farm stand information: (858) 756-3184; Grocery/Market; $$. Situated on 50 acres in the lush backcountry of Rancho Santa Fe, you forget that this little vegetable stand is so close to some of the most expensive housing parcels in the nation. Alice Waters stated in her hugely successful book, Chez Panisse Vegetables, "The Chinos have made an art of farming. For two generations now, they have tended their land with an inexhaustible aesthetic curiosity, constantly searching out new and old varieties of dozens of fruits and vegetables from all over the world, and planting and harvesting year-round." Their produce is trucked to some of the most famous Southern California restaurants on a weekly basis. On any given day, you could be bumping elbows with some of the most brilliant chefs in the local area, all looking for the finest ingredients to prepare unique dishes on their menu. Considered traditional Japanese, the family keeps the secret of successfully growing exotic and organic produce a secret. It may be the best-kept secret next to the Coca-Cola or Kentucky Fried Chicken recipes!

Corner House Cafe & Pizzeria, 11815 Sorrento Valley Road, San Diego, CA 92121; (858) 755-3183; cornerhousecafe.com; American; $. This popular sandwich joint on the corner of Sorrento Valley Road has become famously known for its hot and cold sandwiches, which are served with a signature sweet and sour sauce. The most popular items are the Baja chicken and the Ironman sandwich. The Baja chicken is a hot sandwich, which is made up of grilled chicken breast, jack cheese, grilled onions, jalapeños, tomato, lettuce, and mayonnaise, all served on a French baguette. The Ironman consists of grilled chicken breast, avocado, Swiss cheese, honey mustard, tomato, and sprouts, all inside two soft sourdough slices. Corner House doesn't just stop at sandwiches though; they also serve a mouthwatering specialty burger, fish-and-chips, a great gyro plate, and more. Corner House is located outdoors, which provides beautiful, quaint, tiled tables located on the side patio for customers to enjoy their meal in the quiet scene viewing Sorrento Valley. There aren't many places such as Corner House that serve such a wide menu. The options are just about limitless!

Del Mar Rendezvous, 1555 Camino Del Mar, Del Mar, CA 92014; (858) 755-2669; delmarrendezvous.com; Chinese; $$$. Share unexpected pleasures at this trendy restaurant in Del Mar. The sophisticated atmosphere looks sharp, yet still offers a romantic and upscale ambiance complete with a high-end wine cellar and a beautiful outdoor patio. The most striking part of the decor is the ancient Chinese artwork consisting of traditional pieces and sculptures from China, some dating back 200 years. An open kitchen lends an opportunity to sneak a peek at what options you want cooked up for you from the large 100-plus-item menu. I like to gather with friends and share a variety of spruced-up and exhilarating entrees, such as walnut shrimp, Mongolian rack of lamb, and the wild and crazy banana cheesecake Xango for dessert. In addition, there are over 40 gluten-free and vegetarian options available. Choose from over 20 local, imports, and craft beers, as well as organic, free trade, and sustainably produced teas and coffees, in French presses.

En Fuego Cantina & Grill, 1342 Camino Del Mar, Del Mar, CA 92014; (858) 792-6551; enfuegocantina.com; Mexican; $$$. You'll feel like you're south of the border at this boisterously decorated authentic Mexican eatery that is the longest standing restaurant in Del Mar. Back in the 30s, La Tienda was Del Mar's first hot spot restaurant at this very location. En Fuego Cantina & Grill has respected tradition by pleasing diners with Mexican cuisine, seafood, and tangy margaritas at this 2-story restaurant where you can dine alfresco in covered areas. My favorite part of the restaurant is the indoor La Tienda Wine Room that has been restored to retain the old-style ambiance with old beams and the original 1930s fireplace. En Fuego (loosely translated to "on fire") offers bold flavors from the Mexican Riviera such as Borracho Shrimp sautéed with garlic, tequila, jalapeños, and a touch of cream, or slow roasted Honey Habanero Chicken in a sweet spicy glaze, topped with roasted corn relish.

Gravity Heights, 9920 Pacific Heights Blvd., San Diego, CA 92121; (619) 564-7644; gravityheights.com; Brewpub; $$. Located in Sorrento Mesa, Gravity Heights is a socially inspired 13,000-square-foot brewpub with an expansive outdoor beer garden and full-service restaurant. The menu consists of made from scratch elevated pub fare. Think tuna crudo, chicken wings, dirty fries, burgers, and pizza done right!

International Smoke, 3387 Del Mar Heights Rd., Suite 0100, San Diego, CA 92130; (619) 331-4528; internationalsmoke.com; Steakhouse; $$$$. Located in Del Mar's One Paseo, International Smoke is a chef-driven woodfire cooking experience delivering flavorful smoke infused dishes, and a communal dining environment for locals and visitors alike. The restaurant features shareable dishes and tableside culinary experiences alongside a hand-picked selection of beers on tap and unique cocktails.

Jake's Del Mar, 1660 Coast Blvd., Del Mar, CA 92014; (858) 755-2002; jakesdelmar.com; California Modern; $$$$. Jakes on the water's edge in Del Mar is where you'll want to spend a romantic day or evening with your special someone. The place embodies the coastal living and lifestyle that is envied by anyone outside of Southern California. Where else can you enjoy a meal in the dead of winter and gaze at a multitude of beach activities in the warm sunshine? Take pleasure in upscale beachside eats for lunch, or relax and savor dinner and a dazzling sunset view from the floor- to-ceiling windows. This is clearly one of the more romantic dining venues in the entire city (and the rest of the country, for that matter). Jakes takes full advantage of the ocean's bounty, offering great seafood selections including macadamia nut-crusted salmon; wok char spiced Mahi, sesame wasabi ahi, and grilled shrimp scampi. No visit would be completed without tasting their signature Hula Pie dessert, a frozen treat that is a feast for the eyes and large enough to share with the whole table. Don't Miss Jakes' happy hour, where you can eat and drink at extremely affordable prices; but grab a seat early, as it fills up fast every day of the week!

Ken Sushi, 11375 El Camino Real #120, San Diego, CA 92130; (858) 793-1200; Japanese; $$$. Don't miss this Japanese fusion restaurant in the Carmel Valley neighborhood of San Diego where Chef Ken offers unique sushi roll presentations. Tucked away in an unassuming business park near the I-5 and 56 interchanges is one of the more impressive sushi establishments in Southern California. Working alongside the venerable Chef Ota for years, Ken finally moved into his own place, and called the restaurant exactly what you would expect. Using modern twists that compliment ancient traditions, Ken's Sushi Workshop is a venue to discover new flavors, complimenting some of the freshest seafood available anywhere. The menu prices aren't cheap, but the quality is top-notch.

MARKET Restaurant + Bar, 3702 Via de la Valle, Del Mar, CA 92014; (858) 523-0007; marketdelmar.com; California Modern; $$$$$. This modern and sophisticated restaurant is home to three-time James Beard nominated chef and owner Carl Schroeder, who has garnered so many accolades in the San Diego Dining scene, that quite frankly, it's hard to keep track. The cuisine at this restaurant is so product-driven; it seems to carry a type of pedigree that sets it apart from other restaurants in the area. In fact, when I dine here, I know I've tasted a truly distinctive cuisine from Schroeder's life's work. He's taken his many years of experience, combined with schooling, and paired it with his matchless creativity. It's no wonder that loyal customers and visitors from all over the world keep the place packed on any given night. The menu changes daily depending on Schroeder's whim, or what he's picked up at the farm that day. I co-authored and photographed the Market Restaurant + Bar Cookbook with Schroeder, so you can try your hand at making his famous recipes at home. The book is available for purchase at the restaurant. Reservations are highly recommended.

Mille Fleurs, 6009 Paseo Delicias, Rancho Santa Fe, CA 92067; (858) 756-3085; millefleurs.com; French; $$$$$. Food lovers with an appetite for the lighter side of French know they can count on a true fine dining experience at this restaurant in the village of Rancho Santa Fe. Martin Woesle became chef de cuisine in 1985 and has been impressing customers ever since. The recipient of multiple awards, including Food and Wine's top 25 restaurants in the nation, Mille Fleurs serves French California cuisine in an elegant yet comfortable setting. A daily changing menu for lunch and dinner ensures the freshest and finest ingredients. And since Woesle was born in South Germany, you will see touches from his roots, including the venison rib chop with dried blueberries and hazelnut spätzle or the "wiener schnitzel" of Strauss Farm veal with wild arugula salad, caperberries, and lemon parsley butter.

Milton's, 2660 Via De La Valle, Del Mar, CA 92014; (858) 792-2225; miltonsdeli.com; American; $$. When you walk into Milton's, you will instantly be attracted to the bakery case boasting brownies, cookies, and loads of other goodies. An adjacent meat counter includes deli-style meats such as corned beef, pastrami, and salami. I come here often for the fresh baked bagels, cinnamon raisin, sourdough, and rye breads. The restaurant is casual with white freezer paper for tablecloths and nostalgic pictures on the brick walls. It's easy to imagine you're dining in an old-fashioned New York or Chicago deli. A large menu offers nearly everything you can imagine for breakfast, lunch, and dinner. Where else can you order eggs Florentine or an old-fashioned meat loaf dinner any time of day or night? They are most well-known for large homemade dishes, famous oversize sandwiches, and pub-style foods. A new Chicago-style deep-dish pizza for two has become quite a hit here. As for dessert, my once-a-year indulgence is the German chocolate cake for my birthday. You can buy whole cakes here, or get it by the slice. They also run a very successful catering operation.

Nick & G's, 6106 Paseo Delicias, Rancho Santa Fe, CA 92067; (858) 771-1871; nickandgs.com; Italian; $$$. Nestled in the heart of Rancho Santa Fe, meals at Nick and G's are prepared fresh with local and sustainable ingredients to be enjoyed in a cozy dining room or on a comfortable outdoor patio. Guests can choose from a nice variety of signature flatbreads and pastas, as well as meat and seafood dishes. My favorites are the Calamari Gremolata with lemon caper aioli and checca sauce, Lamb Chops with Polenta and Caramel Carrot Cake for dessert.

North Italia, 3715 Caminito Court Suite 680, San Diego, CA 92130; (858) 252-7720; northitaliarestaurant.com; Italian; $$. Enjoy signature Italian food, including fresh, handmade pasta, pizzas and small plates in a vibrant, welcoming atmosphere. At 5,110 square-feet, North Italia One Paseo boasts a full bar and expansive indoor-outdoor dining room and patio. North Italia creates every dish on its extensive menu with authentic ingredients, consistently delivering quality Italian favorites made from scratch. Choose from an expertly-crafted cocktail menu as well as locally-crafted brews and a variety of red and white wines. A second location is now locted in Fashion Valley at 7055 Friars Road.

Pacifica Del Mar, 1555 Camino Del Mar, Del Mar, CA 92014; (858) 792-0476; pacificadelmar.com; Seafood; $$$$. One of the first modern restaurants to open in the Del Mar Plaza, this local favorite has won awards yearly for its impeccable California cuisine, contemporary style, and stunning views of the Pacific Ocean. Perched on the hill in one of Del Mar's most sought-after locations, Pacifica is one of the most consistent and high-quality seafood restaurants in San Diego. The Ocean Bar is always busy and lively, boasting a selection of at least 150 of the world's finest vodkas, daily specials, and a beautiful aquarium teeming with tropical fish. But it's their creative dishes that take center stage, tugging on all of your senses with colorful arrangements and wonderful aromas and tastes. One of those dishes that has pleased patrons for years is the sugar-spiced salmon, paired with Chinese beans, garlic mashed potatoes, and a subtle mustard sauce that coaxes every bit of flavor out of every ingredient. Nights and weekends are always packed with local and visiting patrons alike, so be sure to make reservations early for the best seating.

Pacific Social, 6025 Village Way, San Diego, CA 92130; (858) 720-6645; cohnrestaurants.com; New American; $$. Food and fun collide at this eatery and bar located within the Village at Pacific Highlands Ranch in Carmel Valley. From the upstairs arcade to the dog-friendly patios with games and a sports-centric bar, this indoor-outdoor restaurant is a vibrant and versatile social hub that caters to its surrounding community. A New American menu with eclectic twists throughout offers classic comfort foods like Chicken Pot Pie and Fish & Chips. Enjoy shared plates as well as internationally inspired dishes like the Mezze Board. Several vegetarian and vegan options are also offered, including the Beyond Burger™. Kids' options include Fried Chicken Tenders with fries and Mac & Cheese.

Poseidon on the Beach, 1670 Coast Blvd., Del Mar, CA 92014; (858) 755-9345; poseidonrestaurant.com; Seafood; $$$$. Think of this place as an island getaway, somewhere to go when you want to relax by the ocean in an up-close and personal way. Large retractable windows create a nice open-air feeling, and an indoor fire pit and lively bar are big draws. Although there is a view from every seat in the house inside the dining room and bar, we prefer to sit on the heated outdoor patio because it feels as though we are basically sitting on the beach itself. This place is great for breakfast, lunch, or dinner. The menu offers a variety of unique salads and sandwiches, as well as grilled meats and seafood. We like to sip on fancy cocktails and munch on tempura-style soft-shell crabs while waiting for the sun to set. A creamy bowl of New England style clam chowder always keeps us nice and warm.

Rubio's, 3545 Del Mar Heights Rd., San Diego, CA 92130; (858) 481-8002; rubios.com; Mexican; $$. No book about San Diego cuisine would be complete without including one of the more famous local culinary success stories. While still a college student, Ralph Rubio frequently visited the local border communities in Mexico for great surfing, entertainment, and snacking at the seaside taquerias. It was there that he first tasted the fish taco, a simple mix of beer-battered local fish, combined with shredded cabbage, salsa, and creamy sauce, all wrapped in a flour tortilla. Inspired (and somewhat obsessed) with his newfound love, he was committed to bringing this taste sensation north of the border. In 1983 Rubio opened his first taco stand in San Diego, centered on this unique combination of ingredients that has now become a national staple for fresh California cuisine available in 5 states spanning the southwest. Now having served over 150 million fish tacos, Rubio's has become synonymous with local cuisine. A trip to one of the many local establishments is a casual experience, with a simple menu of traditional small plates and a self-serve salsa bar featuring a variety of different tastes ranging from mild to extra hot. Next time you're in town, visit this local landmark and enjoy the cuisine that sparked a cultural shift in Southwest American cuisine. Multiple locations can be found throughout San Diego.

Ruth's Chris Steakhouse, 11582 El Camino Real, San Diego, CA 92130; (858) 755-1454; ruthschris.com; Steak House; $$$$. Celebrating 5 decades in business, this modern and well-designed 2-story chophouse, boasting posh white linens and candlelight, continues to please steak worshippers from around the globe. You may think you're a grill master at home, but once you sink your teeth into a Ruth's Chris cut of beef, you may never want to eat a steak anywhere else. Signature, high-quality steaks are seared at 1,800°F, topped with fresh butter, and brought sizzling to your table. Non-steak lovers can opt for the extra-thick lamb chops, cold-water lobster tail with blackening spice, or the oven-roasted free-range double chicken breast stuffed with garlic herb cheese. A deluxe dessert of bread pudding with whiskey sauce is nothing short of exquisite. Additional location is at 1355 N. Harbor Dr, San Diego, CA 92101.

Sbicca, 215 15th St., Del Mar, CA 92014; (858) 481-1001; sbiccadelmar.com; American; $$$$. Loyal customers have been savoring clever modern American cuisine at this lighthearted and friendly neighborhood eatery for many years. Experience a fine dining experience indoors, relax on the casual patio out front, or walk up a little flight of stairs to the covered and heated ocean- view terrace to enjoy a big bowl of lobster bisque. A great happy hour with girl drinks and a bar menu offers anything from coconut calamari with sweet chili glaze to Korean beef lettuce wraps, or crab and lobster cake with cherry tomatoes. The roasted pork prime rib with vanilla yams, bourbon demi-glace and Chantilly cream is a big hit, along with the seared sea scallops. Splurge on the maple-pecan cheesecake with vanilla whipped cream and cranberry-cherry compote for dessert. In addition, Millie's Gelato is a wonderful vegan dessert option that is gluten and dairy free.

Sidecar Doughnuts & Coffee, 3435 Del Mar Heights Rd. Suite D6B, San Diego, CA 92130; (858) 847-2019; sidecardoughnuts.com; Doughnuts; $$. Feel the sweet gratification of warm and delicious doughnuts that are made from scratch daily, using only the finest ingredients possible, and no preservatives. Think fresh and seasonal doughnuts topped with infused glazes, hand crushed compotes, flavored custards and creams, and homemade pie crust and streusel crumble. Doughnuts are fried in small batches every hour, guaranteeing each customer a fresh and warm treat. Flavor selection changes monthly, with a weekly Gluten Free option.

Smashburger, 1555 Camino Del Mar, Del Mar, CA 92014; (858) 461-4105; smashburger.com; Burgers; $$. Feel as though you are on vacation at this Del Mar location resting just steps from the ocean. Walking into Smashburger, you can't help but notice the retro red and white atmosphere that has a definite old-fashioned diner feel. Order your food at the counter up front before grabbing a seat at a booth or table. Choose from the pre-made burger selections or build your own burger from an array of optional toppings and sauces. My favorite is the San Diego burger, which includes their 100 percent fresh Angus beef patty, avocado, cilantro, onions, pepper jack cheese, lettuce, tomato, sour cream, and spicy chipotle mayo. Don't care for a burger? Try a freshly made black bean veggie burger or a crunchy salad. The Sunset salad is my favorite and includes balsamic tomatoes, raisins, dried cranberries, sunflower and pumpkin seeds, as well as blue cheese. If anything, feel the breeze as you sit on the patio right outside the shops and enjoy an icy cold root beer poured over a mountain of vanilla ice cream with a side of sweet potato fries. Multiple locations can be found throughout San Diego.

The Butchery Quality Meats, 3720 Caminito Ct #200, San Diego, CA 92130; (858) 345-1524; butcherymeats.com; Butcher, Sandwiches, Meat Shop; $$. This popular Southern California-based full-service butcher shop, known for high-quality meats, artisan cheeses, craft beers, and wines, is located in San Diego at the One Paseo development in Del Mar. Meat selections include dry-aged and cedar-aged beef, wagyu, all natural pork and poultry, and even exotic options like bison and venison, all of which can be hand-cut to order and prepared to each guest's specifications by skilled butchers. Locally-made sausages, ground beef prepared in-house, and pre-marinated meats are also available, along with a fresh-catch, sustainable seafood selection and deli case stocked with charcuterie and artisan cheeses. In the retail portion of the store, The Butchery carries specialty grocery items like fresh baguettes, seasonings, deli accompaniments, and a curated selection of hard-to-find craft beers and high-end wines that can be expertly paired or suggested by their knowledgeable staff. The Butchery operates four locations in Southern California: Costa Mesa, Brea, Newport Beach-Crystal Cove, and Del Mar.

Thyme in the Ranch, 16905 Avenida De Acacias, Rancho Santa Fe, CA 92091; (858) 759-0747; thymeintheranch.com; Bakery; $$. Nothing beats spending an afternoon driving up a gorgeous tree-lined winding Rancho Santa Fe road and ending up at a bakery's doorstep where the aroma of freshly baked apple pie lures you to come inside. This friendly eatery with small tables scattered about has a simple country charm. Stop in for breakfast and savor quiche by the slice or a warm muffin out of the oven. For lunch, it's a bowl of chili served with a Dutch crunch baguette or old-fashioned turkey meat loaf. Other made-from-scratch goodies include cookies, scones, pies, bread pudding, lemon bars, triple chocolate brownies, and specialty cakes topped with butter cream or whipped cream frosting.

Trattoria Ponte Vecchio, 2334 Carmel Valley Rd, Suite A, Del Mar, CA 92014; (858) 259-9063; pvdelmar.com; Italian; $$$. This exceptional dining destination will remind you of a cozy New York–style Italian restaurant without the hassle of crowded sidewalks, honking taxis, and parking nightmares. Besides, what could be more romantic than a view of the peaceful Torrey Pines Lagoon? There is something wonderful about nestling into a little corner table for two, sharing a bottle of red wine, and rolling pasta from large bowls. Owner Daniel Nobili is always present to greet you in Italian. Old world recipes from his homeland in Milano, Italy, are brought to new life with creative presentations. A specialty of the house is the Spaghetti alla Puttanesca with olives, capers, and anchovies in red sauce; or try the Linguine Ai Frutti Di Mare with mussels, clams, calamari, and shrimp in marinara sauce. Come here and find a little table for two. Call it "Pasta Therapy" for you and a companion!

Urban Plates, 12857 El Camino Real, San Diego, CA 92130; (858) 509-1800; urbanplates.com; American; $$. Fresh off the farm delights in this open kitchen at the Urban Plates in the Del Mar Highlands Town Center. Dine in for lunch or dinner, or take your food home. All the ingredients are conveniently displayed in front of you. Basically, pick out which foods you like best, and your meal is prepared immediately. The menu is divided into a variety of sections. Try the "Carve Up" with barbecue-glazed turkey meat loaf, "Pile Up" with a marinated and grilled wild ono sandwich, or "Load Up" with grilled free-range, cruelty-free chicken. Don't miss Urban Pizzettes made with hand-stretched organic dough as well as the made-from-scratch cream pies, layer cakes, and brownies. Multiple locations can be found throughout San Diego

Venissimo Cheese, 2650 Via De La Valle, Del Mar, CA 92014; (858) 847-9616; venissimo.com; Grocery/Market; $$. With multiple locations in San Diego, this cheese monger hangout in the Flower Hill Mall just off I-5 offers the best cheese varieties from all over the world. You can taste before you buy, and with selections changing daily, you more than likely won't have the same cheese twice. Receipts complete with pronunciations, country of origin, and milk type will make it easier for you to know exactly what you are buying. Accouterments include artisanal breads and crackers, chocolate, olive oil, and more. The staff at Venissimo will also help you design the perfect gift basket or party tray for your next occasion.

Zumbar Coffee and Tea, 10920 Roselle St., San Diego, CA 92121; (858) 622-0000; zumbarcoffee.com; Coffee/Tea; $. Located in the busy tech center of Sorrento Valley, Zumbar is a diminutive shop with a huge reputation for serving some of the best coffee in the area. Taking a craftsman's approach to roasting, they have perfected the process using a vintage, cast-iron coffee roaster situated right behind the ordering counter, giving every patron a chance to see/hear the action. A small selection of pastries and breads are also available, delivered from VG's Donuts and Opera Patisserie every morning. Some regulars believe that the coffee actually advances science, and I have to agree, given the buzzing conversation during my last visit. They also sell fresh-roasted beans at the shop or online, so you're never too far away from a great cup of Joe. Additional location is at 111 Chesterfield Dr, #115, Cardiff, CA 92007.

Escondido, San Marcos, Carmel Mountain Ranch, Rancho Bernardo & Poway

This expansive inland area north of San Diego is rich in history dating back to the early 1800s. Settled in a long valley between coastal mountains, Escondido is surrounded by citrus and avocado groves. Primarily a residential area, neighborhoods include Victorians next to Craftsman bungalows, as well as eclectic Art Deco and post–World War II residences. This city is home to the California Center for the Arts, a facility that attracts over a quarter million visitors from the surrounding area to enjoy musical and cultural events. Be sure to also take a walk on the wild side at the San Diego Zoo Safari Park. Located east in the San Pasqual Valley, it is one of the largest tourist attractions in the San Diego area. With over 1,800 acres of natural enclosures, showcasing more than 400 species of animals, it is visited by over 2 million people every year. San Marcos is considered a centerpiece of higher education in San Diego, as it is home to Palomar College, California State University San Marcos (CSUSM), and several technical schools. For dining, you must visit Old California Restaurant Row. It is North County's largest dining and entertainment center, with 18 restaurants, an Edwards Cinema Complex, and many quaint village boutiques.

Just south of Escondido is the community of Rancho Bernardo, a well-established master-planned community situated along rolling hills and canyons. It is dotted with a number of exclusive country clubs and golf courses, as well as being home to the corporate headquarters for companies like Sony and Hewlett-Packard. The

Bernardo Winery is one of the oldest operating wineries in Southern California, established in 1889 and family owned and operated since 1927.

Carmel Mountain Ranch is situated at the eastern end of the 56 freeway, a newly built feeder highway that directly links the coast and inland areas, from I-5 to I-15. Primarily residential and commercial in nature, it is home to several large shopping centers, easily accessible from the main roads. It is here that you will find a majority of the restaurants, primarily of the chain variety.

Traveling farther south will land you in Poway, nicknamed "The City in the Country." Originally used by the missions as a range for feeding livestock, this area eventually became a centerpiece of agriculture. Although it has become a draw for residential living, Poway is home to the Blue Sky Ecological Reserve, Lake Poway, and many minor hiking and horse riding trails throughout the many canyons. If you're looking for a great picnic spot, Poway offers many options.

©*Maria Desiderata Montana*

A Delight of France, 126 W. Grand Ave., Escondido, CA 92025; (760) 746-2644; adelightoffrance.com; Bakery; $$. This beautiful French bakery and bistro is located right in the center of Escondido on scenic Grand Avenue. Focusing on breakfast and lunch, it has become one of the more popular destinations for locals. Authentic recipes are used throughout the menu. In the morning, most patrons are enjoying one of the many fresh pastries with a cup of coffee, but don't overlook the larger breakfast items. The eggs Benedict is served on a wonderful baked brioche and their strawberry crepes are the best I've tasted. For lunch, try one of the flavorful quiches, or splurge on my favorite, the vol Au vent: a puff pastry shell filled with chicken, mushrooms and curry stew. Sandwiches, Paninis, soups, and salads are also available. Not surprisingly, they offer an extensive assortment of freshly baked cakes and tarts for parties and other special occasions.

AVANT, 17550 Bernardo Oaks Dr., San Diego, CA 92128; (888) 281-7938; ranchobernardoinn.com California; $$$. Located at Rancho Bernardo Inn, AVANT presents a fun and upscale indoor and outdoor ambiance. Diners enjoy sweeping views of the property's award-winning golf course from both indoor and outdoor spaces. Fresh local ingredients make for the perfect wine country dining experienced, with the added benefits of handcrafted classic cocktails, local craft beer, and limited production wines from all over the world. In addition to the regular menu, inventive Off-The-Menu creations are offered nightly. A private demonstration kitchen offers small groups of up to 12 guests direct access to watch the AVANT's chefs in action. Popular menu favorites include Roasted Bone Marrow, Lobster Salad, Hand-Harvested Scallops and Mary's Crispy Chicken. Don't forget to end your meal with a surprise dessert made in limited supply.

Bamboo House, 320 N. Midway Dr., Escondido, CA 92027; (760) 480-9550; bamboohouseca.com; Chinese; $$. Enjoy affordable good-quality food and some very impressive dishes that have lived up to this restaurant's reputation. The dining room, adorned with bright pink tablecloths, is the ideal gathering place for family and friends. A big seller is the deluxe beef, chicken, and shrimp chow mein. The Hong Kong pan-fried egg noodles are heartily paired with barbecue pork, chicken, shrimp, and vegetables. The fillet of sole in black bean sauce melts in your mouth, and the Szechwan pork is spicy good. A great vegetarian option is the braised eggplant and black mushrooms with oyster and soy.

Bellamy's Restaurant, 417 W. Grand Ave., Escondido, CA 92025; (760) 747-5000; bellamysdining.com; California-French; $$$. Bellamy's Restaurant is a hidden gem in Escondido that offers guests an upscale dining experience in a cozy and comfortable atmosphere. Feast on farm to table California Modern cuisine with French influences that include the finest ingredients of local seafood and fresh herbs. Our favorites include the Deep Sea Red Crab Fritters, Moulard Duck Breast, and Soy Lacquered Calamari Steak.

Cafe Luna, 11040 Rancho Carmel Dr., San Diego, CA 92128; (858) 673-0077; cafelunasd.com; Italian; $$$. Cafe Luna is definitely the go-to place for wining, dining, and splurging on pasta dishes galore. Hidden in a strip mall in Carmel Mountain Ranch, just off I-15, this small and comfortable Italian eatery features homemade pastas galore in a European-type setting. Tables are placed close together, making it an ideal romantic dining destination. The signature pasta is the Rosetta, a homemade pasta sheet rolled with ham and Swiss cheese that's sliced and baked with cream and Parmesan cheese. They make delicious spinach-and-cheese-filled ravioli in a light cream sauce, topped with ground walnuts and the fettuccine Bolognese of prime ground filet mignon is as good as the Bolognese that comes out of my Italian kitchen.

Cocina Del Charro, 890 W. Valley Parkway, Escondido, CA 92025; (760) 745-1382; cocinadelcharro.com; Mexican; $$. Praise Baja! For over 30 years there's been Mexican magic in the air at this loud, boisterous, and colorful restaurant in Escondido. A feast for the eyes, as well as the palate, I highly recommend the Cochinita Pibil. A little pocket of flavor, its Mayan-marinated pork cooked in the authentic Yucatan process with achiote and exotic spices, then wrapped in banana leaves and baked. Delving into the fiery Cancun burrito is high-risk behavior. Six large Mexican shrimp are garlic buttered, sautéed, and added to a tomato chipotle sour cream sauce with onions, bell peppers, squash, and rice and stuffed inside a huge flour tortilla, smothered in its own sauce and topped with cheese. Additional restaurant is at 1020 W. San Marcos Blvd, #110, San Marcos, CA 92078.

Decoy Dockside Dining; 1035 La Bonita Dr., San Marcos, CA 92078; (760) 653-3230; lakehousehotelandresort.com; American (New); $$$. This beautiful two-story restaurant is located at the Lakehouse Hotel & Resort on the shores of Lake San Marcos in San Diego's North County. Offering a little something for everyone, Decoy celebrates the unexpected with a New American cuisine that revolves around a wood-burning oven. Seasonal and local ingredients shine in unique creations of Grilled Trumpet Mushroom Salad and Smoked Baby Eggplant. From the farm, don't miss the Rack of Lamb, Duck Breast, or Whole Roasted Mary's Chicken. From the water, popular favorites include Whole Branzino, Rainbow Trout and Maine Lobster.

Edelweiss Bakery, 11639 Duenda Rd., San Diego, CA 92127; (858) 487-4338; edelweissbakerysandiego.com; Bakery; $$. I have two words for this place: "Apple Strudel," the best in town! Offering much more than strudel, Edelweiss has been pleasing guests with these old-world European-style desserts for over 2 decades. From wedding and birthday cakes filled with Bavarian cream and raspberry, to the best-selling German Apple Ring, there isn't a dessert here that I don't crave on a regular basis. Grab a seat and sip on a Kona Blend coffee in one hand and a bear claw in the other. Some other favorites are the English scones, almond raspberry croissants, custard-filled éclairs, and cheese Danish. Chocoholics come here for the chocolate cake with chocolate mousse. I have a soft spot for any Italian pastry, especially the cream- filled cannoli.

Fish House Vera Cruz, 360 Via Vera Cruz, San Marcos, CA 92078; 760-744-8000; fishhouseveracruz.com; Seafood; $$. Deriving its name from the commercial fishing boat the Vera Cruz built in 1965 in Costa Mesa, The Fish House Vera Cruz was born in the historic Old California Restaurant Row in San Marcos in December 1979. As the demand for seasonal and daily-delivered fresh fish selections continued to grow, two new locations were opened in Carlsbad and Temecula. Due to weather, fishing conditions, market availability, and local popularity, fish is subject to availability but can include anything from Atlantic salmon and yellowtail to wahoo, Dorado, or lingcod. In addition to their standard menu, Fish House Vera Cruz features about 15 to 20 different fish daily. Recommended: a big bowl of the Boston-style clam chowder, Pacific oysters from the cold waters of the Northern Pacific, or the rainbow trout from the cool mountain streams of Idaho. All seafood is grilled over a mesquite charcoal grill.

Flippin' Pizza, 342 S. Twin Oaks Valley Rd., San Marcos, CA 92078; (760) 736-3180; flippinpizza.com; Pizza; $$. Flippin' Pizza in San Marcos is the first of the chain of restaurants to include a bar, a chopped salad station, and a spacious interior that's an ideal place for guests to gather. This tasty pizza pie recipe originated in Sicily over 30 years ago, and gained popularity in New York before the concept moved to its San Diego location The Triboro is a favorite, packed with red sauce, meatballs, sausage, and pepperoni. Other styles include plenty of white pie options, as well as calzones and salads. Beer, wine, and a full bar are also available. Multiple locations can be found throughout San Diego.

Mama Kat's Restaurant & Pie Shop, 950 W. San Marcos Blvd., San Marcos, CA 92078; (760) 591-4558; mamakats.com; American; $$. Somewhat hidden in a strip mall along busy San Marcos Boulevard, this simple little eatery has become a haven for locals interested in a hearty breakfast or lunch. The great comfort food you crave is made from scratch here, and the roasted turkey, roast beef, and corned beef are all baked on-site. Reminiscent of an old-fashioned country kitchen, this is one of the best places for early risers to get a filling breakfast and a luscious homemade pie. Savor specialty omelets, Benedicts, pancakes, French toast, and waffles. They are well known for the homemade cream sausage gravy and hollandaise sauce, which are phenomenal when paired with chicken-fried steak or the homemade biscuits. I love the caramel apple Belgian waffle topped with hot apple pie filling and whipped cream. Pies are baked fresh on the premises and include fruit pies, cream pies, and my favorite lemon meringue.

Phil's BBQ, 579 Grand Ave., San Marcos, CA 92078; (760) 759-1400; philsbbq.net; Barbecue; $$$. The secret's in the sauce—the barbecue sauce, that is! Since opening its doors in San Diego in 1998, Phil's BBQ has served over 1 million pounds of barbecue sauce. The long lines waiting for huge portions of Phil's mesquite grilled baby back and beef ribs, chicken, burgers, and sandwiches are well worth it! Pull up a chair at this fun and energetic restaurant where all sides are made from scratch, including the hand-dipped colossal onion rings. By the end of your dining experience you will have something in common with your fellow diners—those paper towels on your table used to wipe the barbecue sauce off your messy hands and faces. Multiple locations can be found throughout San Diego.

Simsim Outstanding Shawarma; 11640 Carmel Mountain Rd Suite 124, San Diego, CA 92128; (858) 618-5948; eatsimsim.com; Middle Eastern; $$. Don't miss this San Diego born fast-casual restaurant with a menu rooted in traditional Middle Eastern cooking. The interior of this 2,400-square-foot space reflects the brand's signature bright and modern design, featuring terrazzo and cork accents, lots of greenery, and ample indoor and outdoor seating. Grill specialties include Lamb Shish Kebob, Chicken Shish Tawook and Beef & Lamb Kebob, all charbroiled, skewered with vegetables and served with a side of rice and Fattoush salad. Signature and from-scratch menu items include its namesake shawarma, plus bowls and sides like the super creamy house made hummus, moutabel and baba ghanoush.

Sushi On The Rock; 16625 Dove Canyon Rd # 108, San Diego, CA 92127; (858) 432-4124; sushiontherock.com; Asian Fusion; $$$. Listen to metro-style music at this high-energy restaurant. Creative and freewheeling sushi masters in the kitchen offer some wild and crazy sushi combinations that will tantalize your taste buds. Customers drive near and far for the salmon and crab stuffed yellow chilies (Dragon Eggs), cooked tempura style and drizzled with wasabi cream sauce. Two dishes that are worthy of prolonged discussion are the jumbo black tiger shrimp, cooked with a sweet and spicy barbecue sauce served over sweet mashed potatoes, and the peppered seared tuna with a sesame ginger ponzu, avocado slices, and red onion. A second location is now open in La Jolla.

The Baked Bear, 11640 Carmel Mountain Rd #120, San Diego, CA 92128; (858) 451-2253; thebakedbear.com; Ice Cream Parlor; $. The Baked Bear is a handcrafted ice cream sandwich parlor offering made-to-order combinations of baked in-house cookies, waffles, brownies and donuts. Don't miss hot fudge sundaes and the Bear Bowl, a warm chocolate chip cookie pie with a scoop of ice cream on top. Multiple locations throughout San Diego.

The Brigantine, 421 W. Felicita Ave., Escondido, CA 92025; (760) 743-4718; brigantine.com; Seafood, $$$. Located near the California Center for the Arts, Escondido, this beautiful restaurant has large dining areas and three connecting patios complete with an ample number of heat lamps for alfresco dining. I personally like to sit inside, with brick walls holding plenty of sea-faring items, and high ceilings to accommodate a tall ship's mast, complete with a rolled-up sail. Guests flock here for the oyster bar featuring several varieties on the half-shell, shooters served in a shot glass with horseradish, and Rockefeller style with spinach, bacon, and Parmesan aioli. If you aren't a fan of oysters, you might want to try the fresh diver scallops Rockefeller. You will get more flavors than you bargained for when you try the lobster relleno poblano chile stuffed with lobster and jack cheese, served with jalapeño white sauce and mango relish. Although this location focuses mainly on seafood, there are a few meat dishes worth noting, such as the slow-roasted prime rib and chicken piccata. Multiple locations can be found throughout San Diego.

The Cork and Craft, 16990 Via Tazon, San Diego, CA 92127; (858) 618-2463; thecorkandcraft.com; New American; $$. With a menu that strikes an edible equilibrium of bar food with steady entrées that attract full-on foodies, the kitchen team at The Cork and Craft is changing the way people think about dinner. This chef-driven restaurant is located inside Abnormal Wine and Beer Co. (Abnormal Company is San Diego's first and only restaurant, winery and brewery in one). The fresh and seasonal menu features

Modern California cuisine with an emphasis on French technique. The large dining room features an open-air kitchen where guests can see the culinary team at work. The restaurant ambiance is relaxed and comfortable, however the cuisine is prepared with an unexpected sophisticated twist and approachable price point that would rank at any upscale restaurant.

The Grand Tea Room, 145 W. Grand Avenue, Escondido, CA 92025; (760) 233-9500; thegrandtearoom.com; American/Tea; $$$. Here's a concept that you don't see very often, especially in our busy, electronic-focused world: a full-service tearoom offering traditional teas and snacks that will transport you to a simpler time. Get your friends together and enjoy the slow life. Although you can walk in any time and order from the a la carte menu, I strongly suggest you call ahead and reserve a traditional afternoon tea, including a table for 2 hours to enjoy 4 to 5 courses and freshly steeped tea. Your meal includes soup, assorted tea sandwiches, seasonal fresh fruit, scones, and petite desserts. Casual business attire is the most common practice, but on many days, you will also find some guests wearing tea dresses with hats and gloves. There are three times available Tuesday through Saturday, so be sure to call ahead.

The Habit Burger Grill, 727 W San Marcos Blvd, San Marcos, CA 92078; (760) 891-0542; habitburger.com; Burgers; $. This fast-casual restaurant specializes in preparing 100% fresh and never frozen made-to-order ground beef burgers grilled over an open flame. The menu also includes hand-cut salads, grilled sandwiches, onion rings, sweet potato and French fries, and tasty shakes and malts. Multiple locations can be found throughout San Diego.

Vincent's, 113 W. Grand Ave., Escondido, CA 92025; (760) 745-3835; vincentsongrand.com; French; $$$$. It is through the inspiration of the seasons that makes me want to call the food here "French a la California style" at this historic downtown Escondido restaurant. Diners clamber to get a table here to taste the many delicacies. Dip your bread into the steamed local Carlsbad Aqua farm mussels in herbs, garlic, white wine, and cream, while you wait for half of a roasted Maple Leaf Farm duckling prepared in a candied-orange and crystallized-ginger sauce, served with potato gratin and a medley of seasonal vegetables. Having been honored with the "Award of Excellence" from the Wine Spectator many times over, there isn't a wine you won't discover and love from the massive on-site wine cellar.

Kearny Mesa, Mira Mesa & Clairemont

In the early 1900s this land was initially purchased as a ranch by newspaper tycoon Edward Scripps, who longed for an escape from the hectic East Coast but didn't want to settle in the downtown San Diego area. Most of the existing developments were built in the post-war boom of the 1950s as one of the primary residential areas for the military, since the Naval Air Station was nearby. Now called the Marine Corps Air Station Miramar, this military base became famous as the backdrop for Top Gun, an extremely popular movie starring Tom Cruise.

Highly industrialized, most of the main thoroughfares are lined with commercial property. This area was one of the first in San Diego to include fully designed suburban neighborhoods, with many city amenities included in the overall layout. Much of the land has been developed, except for San Clemente, Los Penasquitos, and Tecolote Canyon Parks. These are great areas to hike or bike along the natural canyons and imagine what most of San Diego looked like before modernization.

More so than any other area of the city, you will find large pockets of Asian cultures, including Chinese, Japanese, Korean, Thai, and Vietnamese. Convoy Street is a great example of this ethnic influence, with a large concentration of authentic restaurants and markets. Oftentimes, you'll know the cuisine is good because a majority of the patrons are local and speak the language most appropriate for the location. Many of the menus will also be written in both native language and English. In general, the prices are very reasonable, any time of day. The markets can be a fun experience, as you will find aisle upon aisle of exotic spices, packaged foods, and fresh items not found in a normal grocery store.

BUGA Korean B.B.Q. 5580 Clairemont Mesa Blvd., San Diego, CA 92117; (858) 560-1010; bugabbq.com; Korean; $$$. This Korean barbecue restaurant has a successful business based on quality ingredients and authentic recipes. Prices for dinner are higher than many comparable eateries in San Diego, but this is reflective of their choice to use Kobe and Neiman Ranch beef. There's always something special and delicious about natural meats that avoid hormones or antibiotics, and this is reflected in every dish. Two of my favorite barbecue dinners are the Joomuluck (boneless rib) and Seng Deung Shim (rib eye). For something truly authentic, choose one of the stews or hot pot casseroles. Reasonably priced lunch specials are available during the week. The spacious dining room can accommodate a good crowd; so, finding a table is easier than many smaller restaurants in the area.

China Max, 4698 Convoy St., # 101, San Diego, CA 92111; (858) 650-3333; chinamaxsd.com; Chinese; $$. I like to call this "pish-posh white tablecloth" Cantonese seafood and New Hong Kong–style cuisine, which will have you so addicted; the staff may have to pry you out of your chair to get you to leave. It's a little pricey for a Chinese place, but when you walk in and smell the fresh spices wafting out of the kitchen, you'll spare no expense. Seriously good eats include the daily dim sum and the light and crispy fried baby squid with a touch of garlic salt. The sizzling beef with black bean sauce will warm your bones, and you can actually order live seafood from their tank, including Boston lobster, scorpion fish, sheepshead fish, and abalone. Don't miss the mango pudding for dessert. Beer, wine, and sake are always available.

Di-Chan Thai Restaurant, 5535 Clairemont Mesa Blvd., San Diego, CA 92117; (858) 569-0084; dichanthaifood.com; Thai; $$. Enjoy delicious and authentic Thai dishes at Di-Chan Thai (translation: My Thai Restaurant) that's been around for over 20 years. The restaurant is a small hole-in-the-wall offering honest portions that are not only flavorful but healthy too! While vegetarians have their choice of vegetables and fish entrees, carnivores can opt for beef, chicken, and pork. All dishes are cooked to order, and you can order your food any way you like. Don't miss the Pad see-ew, the spicy basil fried rice with shrimp, or the pad Thai.

Farmer's Table, 3057 Clairemont Dr., San Diego, CA 92117; (619) 359-4485; myfarmerstable.com; New American; $$. Farmer's Table offers innovative spins on time-tested favorites, adding a second location to its original outpost in La Mesa. Housed in a 3,500 square-foot space located along Clairemont Drive, the Bay Park space touts charming farm-inspired décor indicative of the restaurant's farm-to-fork focus, including upcycled fixtures such as a repurposed tractor, rustic wooden crates filled with greenery, old magazines curated into eclectic collages, and refurbished wood showcased throughout the space. Featuring local flavors sourced from San Diego's farming and sustainable food communities, Farmer's Table specializes in dishes with integrity; an important and defining element of San Diego's environmentally-conscious population. Multiple locations throughout San Diego.

Hidden Fish; 4764 Convoy St. Ste A, San Diego, CA 92111; (858) 210-5056; hiddenfishsushi.com; Sushi; $$$. With only 13 seats, this omakase-only sushi restaurant allows guests to take part in an intimate dining experience. Executive Sushi Chef and owner John Hong (Chef Kappa) offers "timed dining" where he and his team create inventive daily menus, allowing guests to try a variety of sushi pieces and taste new combinations. Omakase, a phrase which translates directly to 'I'll leave it up to you,' is a traditional Japanese style of dining where patrons place their full trust in the chef to present innovative and delicious dishes. A rotating selection direct from Japan's renowned Tsukiji Fish Market ensures that each ingredient has been selected by experts for quality and freshness. Chef Kappa's culinary passion stems from early childhood, and further developed as he learned from sushi masters and educators. After experiencing high-end and expensive omakase restaurants in Los Angeles and New York, Kappa created Hidden Fish, reinventing the idea to be affordable and available. Before or after a meal, diners are also invited to relax in the lounge for a glass of beer, wine or sake. The lounge is standing-room only and reflects the intimacy of the sushi bar.

Jasmine Seafood Restaurant, 4609 Convoy St., #A, San Diego, CA 92111; (858) 268-0888; jasmineseafood.com; Chinese; $$. This is an extremely large and casual restaurant that resembles a dining hall where live seafood chosen from any of the 6 tanks in the restaurant is prepared Cantonese style. Live fish changes daily and includes lobster and crab. Choose from a large menu of authentic fare, including noodle and barbecue specialties, as well as duck, squab, pork, beef, and chicken dishes. The specialty of the house is the Cantonese-style roast duck, which serves 4 people. The big draw here is the Cantonese-style dim sum brunch, served daily. Choose from over 50 intricate mini-dishes presented on steamed carts and brought right up to your table. Try the barbecue pork bun, the stuffed crab claws, and the fried shrimp balls—or, if you're brave enough, the chicken feet! Weekends are very busy, so come early.

Khan's Cave Grill & Tavern, 350 Clairemont Mesa Blvd., Suite F, San Diego, CA 92123; (858) 279-9799; khanscave.com; Asian/Fusion; $$. This hidden jewel in North County is located in a small strip mall with convenient parking nearby. The interior is quite spacious and can accommodate happy hour partiers as well as diners seeking a more intimate dining venue. A heated patio is also a nice option for guests wishing to dine outdoors. The focal point is a bar with over 20 local and international beers on tap, as well as plenty of wine choices. The diverse menu includes an impressive variety, including exotic Asian fusion tapas. The best strategy is to order a few items and share with your dining partners, as this guarantees you'll get to experience various flavor combinations. One of the house specialties is the Chilean sea bass with steamed vegetables and a choice of garlic ginger or black bean sauce. Also, be sure to try the Mongolian lamb shank, super-tender meat that abounds nicely with a mildly sweet sauce and vegetables. One of my all-time favorites is the spicy eggplant in Kung Pao sauce, served over rice.

Mignon Pho + Seafood , 3860 Convoy St., San Diego, CA 92111; (858) 278-0669; mignonpho.com; Vietnamese; $$. Fabulous food and colorful dishes make for amazing memories at this modern, yet comfortable eatery in the Sunrise Plaza. Genuine Vietnamese family recipes, passed down from generations, are served in generous portions meant for sharing. The pho (beef broth noodle) is made from the bone marrows of large beef bones. Each bowl of pho comes with your choice of three ingredients and a side dish of vegetable. I like to order this big bowl of savory goodness with beef meatballs (bo vien), shrimp balls, and soft tofu. For guests who are sensitive to gluten, their brown rice noodles are 100 percent gluten free. Other popular favorites include the fried chicken wings tossed in fish sauce and the refreshing julienne green papaya salad. The servers here will educate you on soju, a distilled beverage native to Korea. Drop soju into a pint of draft beer, or vice versa for some real fun!

Opera Patisserie, 9254 Scranton Rd., San Diego, CA 92121; (858) 458-9050; operacafe.com; Bakery; $$. Find a safe haven in this museum of French food specials written on a chalkboard, including salads, sandwiches, crepes, soups, and house specialties. The carefully made croque monsieur, a French style grilled cheese sandwich with Gruyere cheese, béchamel sauce and Black Forest ham has a gratifying charred and chewy texture. Another popular favorite is the vegetarian quiche, a French-style custard pie filled with oven- roasted tomatoes, sautéed spinach, feta cheese, and fresh buffalo mozzarella. Ambitious desserts of raspberry mascarpone mousse, a luscious pastry made with pistachio strawberry pomegranate, and my favorite gluten-free chocolate lava cake.

Pho Ca Dao & Grill, 8373 Mira Mesa Blvd., San Diego, CA 92126; (858) 564-0917; phocadaogrill.com Vietnamese; $. Pho Ca Dao is a spacious and colorful dining room that is packed for lunch and dinner. However, service is quite prompt, so tables turn over very quickly. The quality and price are really unbeatable, with many items less than $5. The seafood pho and the broken rice dishes are excellent. Multiple locations can be found throughout San Diego.

Phuong Trang, 4170 Convoy Street, San Diego, CA 92111; (858) 565-6750; phuongtrangrestaurant.com; Vietnamese; $$. You don't want to miss this authentic Vietnamese restaurant in Convoy Plaza. An extremely large menu boasts appetizers, soups, noodle dishes, and main courses including chicken, beef, pork, and seafood as well as vegetarian entrees. Your palate will remember the oodles of noodles in the broth-based vegetable Bun Nuoc, a warm vermicelli noodle soup served with shredded red cabbage, bean sprouts, jalapeño peppers, fresh mint, and lime. Two real highlights are the oven-roasted whole catfish served with vegetables, fish sauce, and rice paper or the Dungeness crab plucked live from the tank, then lightly battered and fried and tossed with garlic, salt, pepper, red bell peppers, and scallions. Okay, one more—the locals know to come here for the strawberry or Key lime ice-cream pie for dessert!

Rakiraki Ramen & Tsukemen, 4646 Convoy St., #102-A, San Diego, CA 92111; (858) 573-2400; rakirakiramen.com; Ramen; $$. Located the heart of Kearny Mesa and open since 2012, the lines out the door are proof enough that the ramen here is worth the wait! Diners take their seats in an ultra-chic space beneath Japanese lanterns. An up-to-the-minute open kitchen allows diners to watch the chefs in action preparing succulent bowls of ramen "aburi" style, complete with novel toppings. Sip on a Japanese sake and enjoy the Original Signature Ramen with handcrafted noodles and original chicken broth topped with bamboo shoots, green onions, organic crushed sesame, wakame seaweed and your choice of aburi organic chicken or aburi chasiu. Other authentic Japanese dishes include starters, salads, specialty rolls, curry, tsukemen, dipping noodles, ramen burgers and rice bowls. Additional locations throughout San Diego.

Robata Ya Oton, 5447 Kearny Villa Rd., Suite D, San Diego, CA 92123; (858) 277-3989; Japanese; $$. Just look for the crowd hanging out at the open bar watching the chefs in action, and you'll know you've arrived at one of the finest Japanese restaurants in town. This is prime territory to experience exotic Japanese cuisine in your own private booth, a cozy setting that's conducive to hand holding and kissing, as well as eating, of course. Take your shoes off before you step into your booth where you sit on mats placed on a bench close to the table. It's almost as if you are sitting on the floor, but you're not. The Shabu-Shabu allows you to cook your own food, at your own pace, and to your own liking, adding sliced beef, tofu, and assorted vegetables over a pot of boiling water, seasoned with kelp. If you want to leave the cooking to the master chefs, try the Kakuni braised Kurobuta pork, or the Tara no Saikyo Yaki, grilled marinated black cod with miso flavor.

Sher E Punjab, 9254 Scranton Rd., Ste. #102, San Diego, CA 92121; (858) 458-2858; sherepunjabsd.com; Indian; $$. Located in a strip mall, this cozy Indian getaway offers a family-friendly atmosphere and a menu filled with Indian favorites. There are multiple platters of vegetarian, chicken, lamb, tandoori, and seafood specialties. With your meal, it is suggested that you order the homemade naan, plain bread, which is absolutely delectable and melts in your mouth. I recommend the lassi, a popular mango yogurt smoothie, which goes well with just about any dish in the restaurant. Sher E Punjab offers an all-you-can-eat buffet on Friday and Saturday nights, allowing you to choose from all of the favorites. The buffet contains appetizers, salads, rice, a variety of delicious curries, and dessert.

Siam Nara, 8993 Mira Mesa Blvd., San Diego, CA 92126; (858) 566-1300 siamnara.com; Thai; $$. Before you know it, you are pursuing the exotic cuisine at Siam Nara, a fine dining restaurant with a menu that spans a myriad of Thai cuisine specialties, including starts, soups, rice, noodles, and more. From the culture to the cooking, customers know this is as authentic as Thai food gets. Once the dishes start rolling, each one looks more like an edible work of art. I like the goong num pla wan. Eaten the during winter months, when the nem flowers (dork sadao) and river prawns become plentiful, beautiful prawns are grilled and served with tamarind sauce (num pla wan), roasted shallots, and Thai chili. Another off-the-grid standout is the crispy golden sole fillet topped with five signature sauces: pineapple puree, roasted garlic, and a trio of chili sauces. Dotted with kaffir lime leaves, it is a sweet and spicy Thai favorite.

Studio Diner, 4701 Ruffin Rd., San Diego, CA 92123; (858) 715-6400; studiodiner.com; American; $$. Featured on the Food Network's Diners, Drive-ins, and Dives, this eye-catching, neon-lighted diner continues to turn heads. It's nearly impossible to miss this place after the sunsets. Take a trip back to the 1940s where food was simple and the menu was easy to read. With a flashy, domed ceiling and movie-making equipment throughout the dining room, you'll feel reenergized at this 24-hour hot spot. No fluff, just good, down-home burgers and fries, hot dogs, sandwiches, fried clams, and maybe even a Bud Light with a warm Julian apple pie a la mode. One of my sinful indulgences for breakfast is the chicken-fried steak and eggs, with hash browns and toast. Or try their Grip Burger, a half-pound cheeseburger you might have a hard time finishing. Low-carb dieters will appreciate being able to order their burgers "protein style," substituting buns for leaves of lettuce.

The Godfather, 7878 Clairemont Mesa Boulevard, Suite G, San Diego, CA 92111; (858) 560-1747; godfatherrestaurant.com; Italian; $$$. From the moment you enter this dimly lit landmark, you know you're in for a special treat. Since its opening in 1974, The Godfather has been considered one of the finest authentic Italian restaurants in Southern California. Tucked away in a neighborhood widely known for its Asian influences, this deeply Sicilian eatery has defied the odds. Don't look for any fusion dishes or modern music and decor. Here you will find comfortable booths, cloth-laden tables, tuxedo-clad servers, and soft music from a live piano filling the air. Upon your arrival, fresh baked bread and lightly breaded zucchini slices are placed on your table. The wine list is impressive and chock-full of excellent Italian varietals. Equally stunning is the menu, a comprehensive tour of the finest Italian dishes and suggested wine pairings, making your decision all the more difficult. Must-haves are the linguine ai frutti di mare, a medley of the sea mounded over pasta, and the cannelloni medaglione, pasta shells filled with filet mignon, Sicilian marsalla wine, and fresh mushrooms. Be sure to save a little room for the house-made Tiramisu, one of the best in the city. A large banquet room is also available for private parties. Dinner reservations are highly recommended.

The Original Sab-E-Lee, 6925 Linda Vista Rd B, San Diego, CA 92111; (858) 650-6868; originalsab-e-lee.webs.com; Thai; $$. Opened since 2008, this tiny understated eatery in Linda Vista offers authentic Isaan (northeastern) style Thai cuisine at reasonable prices. Choose from delicious appetizers, soups, salads, meat, and vegetable entrees, and noodle and rice dishes. I am a big fan of the curries, which can be made as spicy as you like. My favorite is the moist garlic and red chili-based curry made with bamboo shoots and eggplant. All curries are served with a choice of beef, pork, chicken, vegetable, or tofu. Don't worry, if your mouth feels like it's on fire, cool it down with a Thai ice tea or the "Sweet Sticky Rice with Mango." You won't be disappointed. Additional location is at Rancho Penasquitos Towne Center, 13223 Black Mountain Rd, San Diego, CA 92129.

The WineSellar & Brasserie, 9550 Waples St., Ste. 115, San Diego, CA 92121; (858) 450-9557; winesellar.com; California French; $$$. In a modest location on a corner in Sorrento Mesa, there is a wine cellar and a brasserie under the same roof. The WineSeller, located on the ground floor, offers domestic and international wines from around the world. They hand-select wines that possess special character and quality. Find a great wine at a reasonable price, or go for the gusto with an expensive collector's wine. Located up a short flight of stairs, the Brasserie offers impeccable dinner service matched with artful plates of innovative California French cooking based on homemade, seasonal, and locally grown ingredients. Choose the Kurobato Pork "Two Ways" with Tomatillo, Date, Orange and Cocoa or the Hamachi Tataki with Meyer Lemon Puree, Parsley, Radish and Togarashi. For dessert it's none other than the Fig Tart Le Pastourelle.

Wa Dining Okan, 3860 Convoy St., #110, San Diego, CA 92111; (858) 279-0941; wa-dining-okan.cafes-world.com; Japanese; $$. You can taste the history and the culture of the people through the food at Wa Dining Okan where, through their own independent channels, they import seasonal ingredients direct from various areas in Japan to prepare a true Japanese cuisine that will leave you completely fulfilled. From a variety of Japanese casseroles to rice cooked in a "Kama" Kettle, the ingredient-driven menu rivals the best at this small, all-occasion restaurant. If you're lucky enough to get a seat at this small restaurant, this is a great place to enjoy your tapas while mingling with the staff. Twelve different tapas rotate daily, and are served in the dining room as well, and include bean starch noodle salad, Japanese potato and macaroni salads, fried eggplant with spicy miso sauce, deep fried tofu with Japanese gravy, simmered pumpkin in broth, boiled asparagus mixed with miso and vinegar. Other worldly and daring dishes include roasted bonito sashimi, beef tongue steak and egg omelet with eel. Open for lunch and dinner. Reservations recommended.

Yokohama Yakitori Koubou, 3904 Convoy Street, Suite 108, San Diego, CA 92111; (858) 277-8822; yokohamayakitorikoubou.com; Japanese; $. Tucked away in an area of San Diego filled with Asian choices, this unassuming Japanese restaurant is an excellent choice. The semicircular bar and small dining room decorated with dark woods is frequently occupied with locals enjoying authentic food and conversation. An open kitchen allows you to watch the chefs slicing and dicing various meats and vegetables for skewers grilled over traditional Japanese bincho charcoal. Plenty of other rice and noodle dishes are also available. A unique dish is the Nippon no nikomi, a Japanese-style meat and vegetable stew cooked in a fish base. Be sure to also try their excellent selection of hot or cold sake and soju.

La Jolla

La Jolla is home to some of the most affluent residents in the area. And for good reason: It is culturally dense, packed with high-end, ocean-view restaurants, 4-star hotels, art galleries, boutiques, and lots of shopping. Although the geography stretches from beaches to rolling residential hillsides, it is the small area nearest the natural cove that garners the most interest from visitors. Considered one of the most beautiful (and photographed) beaches in Southern California, the La Jolla Cove includes a couple of small swimming beaches, a grassy picnic area, and high bluffs with the waves crashing into foam during high tide. The popular underwater park is a haven for swimmers, scuba divers, and snorkelers of all skill levels. The area is also frequented by packs of sea lions that lie on the beach and nearby rocks, and sea birds of all kinds, including gulls and pelicans. Prospect Street runs along the coast and is lined with various eateries and hotels that have some of the best views (and food) in San Diego.

La Jolla Shores is just a short walk north of the cove, and has a long stretch of beach lined with a boardwalk until it intersects with the Scripps Pier. Drive a few miles north up a steep hillside, and you'll find yourself at the entrance to the Torrey Pines Reserve, with extensive walking paths and nature trails. Farther east is UC San Diego and more shopping at University Towne Center and other nearby commercial centers.

A.R. Valentien, 11480 N. Torrey Pines Rd., La Jolla, CA 92037; (858) 777-6635; arvalentien.com; French; $$$$. The Lodge at Torrey Pines is home to A.R. Valentien, one of San Diego's most notable and refined restaurants. You will certainly feel transported whiling away the hours in a charming dining room with a beautiful view of the Torrey Pines Golf Course and the Pacific Ocean just off the bluffs in the distance. Classically French-trained, with more than 30 years of experience, Executive Chef Jeff Jackson offers a temple of flavor in his market-driven cuisine from some of California's finest organic farms, orchards, and fishermen. The menu revolves around the seasons, assuring superb freshness and taste with every bite. The charcuterie section of the menu is one of my favorites, offering Duck and Pistachio Pâté with pickled fig, frisee and whole grain mustard. Artisanal and farmhouse cheeses are outstanding, and the meat and seafood options range anywhere from lobster and swordfish to duck, Niman Ranch pork loin, and dry aged rib eye steak. The Quince Steamed Pudding with poached cranberries, pecan Florentine and vanilla ice cream is worth writing home about.

Barbarella, 2171 Avenida De La Playa, La Jolla, CA 92037; (858) 454-7373; barbarellarestaurant.com; Italian; $$$. This simple and stylish mainstay in La Jolla is the perfect dining venue for guests wanting to feel as though they have stepped into a charming, modern, California-style bistro with a Mediterranean-inspired menu. Offering indoor and outdoor seating, Owner Barbara Beltaire thinks of this place as her home, where her staff takes an honest approach to organic and seasonal food by allowing the flavors to express themselves in simple and fresh ways. An engaging crowd of tourists and after-work locals know to come here for the French onion soup with melted Gruyere and the fresh organic salmon tartare. For diners craving Italian fare, Beltaire does Italian right with a variety of delicious pizzas and baked orecchiette pasta with Gorgonzola, pecorino, Parmesan, and pancetta in a light cream sauce. In addition, if you have a hungry pooch, a special Doggie Menu will do the trick!

Beaumont's, 5662 La Jolla Blvd., La Jolla, CA 92037; (858) 459-0474; beaumontseatery.com; California Modern; $$$. Located in the Bird Rock Community of La Jolla, this down-to-earth restaurant has customers lining up for progressive American cuisine paired with live music on select nights, as well as a "Blues Brunch." Whether you want to sample exclusive appetizers or take a voyage through some incredible meat, seafood, and pasta courses, Beaumont's proves ideal. From gutsy duck confit tacos and pork chile relleno to rustic prime short ribs bourguignon or roasted chicken pappardelle, Beaumont's expertly prepared cuisine is a mainstay for diners seeking unforeseen flavors. Signature martinis and hazelnut gelato bon bons for dessert further bolster the allure!

BJ's Restaurant Brewhouse, 8785 Villa La Jolla Dr, La Jolla, CA 92037, (858) 257-3640, bjsrestaurants.com; New American; $$. Diners come here for the handcrafted beer and the Chicago-style pizza with a Southern California twist. Don't miss their famous Pizookie for dessert! Multiple locations can be found throughout San Diego.

Bernini's Bistro, 7550 Fay Ave, La Jolla, CA 92037; (858) 454-5013; berninisbistrolajolla.com; Italian; $$. Start your day with lemon ricotta pancakes or opt for a fresh salad, sandwich, or burger for lunch. For dinner, start with the pistachio crusted shrimp appetizer with grilled pineapple and mango teriyaki aioli. A large array of meat and seafood offerings is also available as well as woodfired pizza and pasta selections.

Bistro du Marché by Tapenade, 7437 Girard Ave., La Jolla, CA 92037; (858) 551-7500; bistrodumarche.net; French; $$$. While this isn't a 'maison' located in France, it might as well be. Award-winning Chef Jean Michel Diot has done something right, because when you dine here, you'll feel like you're in a refined Parisian bistro. Since 1998, Diot has been a magician in the kitchen, combining traditional French techniques with natural aromatic ingredients to create simple, yet classic dishes. Eating authentic is easy with the burgundy escargots with fresh herbs and garlic butter. Wild game lovers should try the Roasted Duck Breast with Truffle Mashed Potatoes, Brussel Sprouts, Truffle and Port Sauce or the Venison Loin with Huckleberry and Burgundy sauce. Having an affinity for Italian food and those rich French sauces, I especially like the Wild Mushroom Ravioli with Port Cream Sauce and Parmigiano Reggiano. With so many French options, you will definitely need more than one visit!

Brockton Villa, 1235 Coast Blvd., La Jolla, CA 92037; (858) 454-7393; brocktonvilla.com; American; $$$. Originally a historic La Jolla cottage built in 1894, Brockton Villa is now the locals' go-to for the view of the ocean, the barking seals on the seashore, and of course, the coastal-inspired fresh catch seafood cuisine. Both the dining room and open-air patio face the incredible shoreline and famous seaside cliffs where waves continuously crash against the rocks. Simple, flavorful, and seasonal, the menu includes a richly decadent clam chowder or lump blue crab cake sliders for lunch that never disappoint. There is no better location for a romantic dinner, watching the sunset over the Pacific, and enjoying savory meals over a candlelit table. The hours linger nicely with oysters "Brockafeller," fiery dill shrimp butter leaf wraps, and almond-chili–crusted scallops. Not just for breakfast, top off your meal with their legendary Coast Toast served "a la mode" with cinnamon or vanilla gelato.

Burger Lounge, 1101 Wall St., La Jolla, CA 92037; (858) 456-0196; burgerlounge.com; Burgers; $$. A healthy and delicious burger does exist! Say goodbye to conventionally grown beef, and hello to hormone- and antibiotic-free beef that comes from one farm where the animals' diet consists of tall green grass from a Kansas prairie. You'll get a flavorsome burger sandwiched between a soft, organic whole-wheat bun made with a little unbleached white flour and blackstrap molasses, organic white cheddar or American cheese, fresh or grilled onion, tomato, and house-made Thousand Island sauce. Non-beef lovers can opt for a veggie burger made with quinoa, salmon, or all-natural turkey, or choose a green salad topped with grilled or crispy chicken breast. French fries and onion rings are cooked in 100 percent refined peanut oil. Splurge on the chocolate malt or the ginger beer float with vanilla ice cream. Draft beer and wine are available. Multiple locations can be found throughout San Diego.

Café Milano, 711 Pearl St, La Jolla, CA 92037, (858) 454-3806, cafemilanolajolla.com; Italian; $$. Enjoy Northern Italian cuisine of breads, pastas, and desserts in a cozy dining room or garden patio. Popular menu favorites include spaghetti Bolognese and eggplant parmigiana. Don't miss the flute limoncello for dessert; a refreshing lemon gelato decorated with a limoncello swirl, presented in an elegant champagne glass.

Caroline's Seaside Café, 8610 Kennel Way, La Jolla, CA 92037; (858) 202-0569; grnfc.com/carolines/; American; $$. Nestled on the water's edge of the UCSD Scripps Institute of Oceanography Seaside Forum, just steps north of the La Jolla Shores beach, stands this simple and contemporary eatery. Guests are welcome to enjoy healthy and creative California-style cuisine for breakfast or lunch while soaking up the endless ocean views extending far beyond Scripps Pier. The outdoor patio boasts a bistro-style charm and is the perfect place to dine alfresco, soaking up the warm sun under a tall terrace, complete with an up-close and personal view of the grand Pacific.

Catania, 7863 Girard Ave #301, La Jolla, CA 92037; (858) 551-5105; cataniasd.com; Italian; $$$. The smell of wood-fired pizzas hits you as you walk in the door at Whisknladle Hospitality's Catania, nestled on the top floor of the La Plaza center in La Jolla, California. Inspired by Whisknladle Hospitality Owner Arturo Kassel and Culinary Director/Partner Ryan Johnston after their two-week, 1,400-mile road trip through Italy, this innovative 3,750-square-foot restaurant, with an expansive patio and outdoor bar space, puts diners right near the ocean and within walking distance of shopping. Enjoy Italian coastal cuisine on a whole new level. Don't miss the Whole Roasted Branzino with manila clams, spring onion pesto, grilled asparagus and chili bread crumbs or the Wild Boar Corzetti with cherries, pine nuts, aged balsamic, honey, gremolata and Parmesan. Exciting desserts include Limoncello Tiramisu and Semifreddo with Nutella, hazelnut, olive oil and Saba.

Chedi Thai, 737 Pearl St., #110, La Jolla, CA 92037; (858) 551-8424; chedithaibistro.com; Thai; $$$. Executive Chef, Restaurant Designer, and Owner Sutharin Pia Kampuntip cooks traditional Thai cuisine prepared in a more contemporary way at this enchanting and attractively decorated eatery on Prospect Street. Since each dish on the menu boasts its own unique twist, order multicourses to share. Great starters are the Thai crispy calamari cooked in sweet roasted chili sauce, crispy corn cakes served with cucumber relish, or the steamed vegetable dumplings generously stuffed with shiitake mushrooms, corn, tofu, and spinach. The pad Thai rice noodles mingle deliciously with shrimp, eggs, bean sprouts, tofu, and chopped peanuts in a tamarind sauce. Most impressive of all is the crispy and boneless red snapper with cherry tomatoes and bok choy in a three-flavor sauce. A daily happy hour is a great way to try many dishes at an affordable price.

©Maria Desiderata Montana

Cody's La Jolla, 8030 Girard Ave, La Jolla, CA 92037; (858) 459-0040; codyslj.com; American; $$. A cozy cottage and beach-inspired ambiance attracts the locals here. For breakfast think crispy fried chicken served with homemade buttermilk biscuits and cracked pepper and onion gravy. For lunch, the lobster roll is stuffed in griddled brioche, lightly tossed in butter and aioli, and served with hand-cut French fries and cole slaw.

Come On In Café, 11011 N. Torrey Pines Road, La Jolla, CA 92037; (858) 412-6135; comeonincafe.com; American; $. It's all about freshness and flavor at this cozy neighborhood bistro for breakfast, lunch and dinner. The coffee and pastries alone are worth the trip! Additional locations throughout San Diego.

Crab Catcher, 1298 Prospect St., La Jolla, CA 92037; (858) 454-9587; crabcatcher.com; Seafood; $$$$. With spectacular ocean views throughout the dining room and outdoor patio, the Crab Catcher specializes in California and Pacific Rim–inspired seafood selections. Be sure to schedule your visit when you can enjoy the scenery and colorful sunsets, as the dark of night will limit your sight line. I am a sucker for a great Crab Louie, and in my opinion, they serve the best in town! With a blend of crabmeats, mixed field greens, tomatoes, cucumber, avocado, and special dressing, it's priceless. Other specialties include savory crab cakes, crab-stuffed mushrooms, king crab ceviche, and Maryland blue crab wontons. Of course, they serve plenty of other offerings from both land and sea, so be sure to bring your sunglasses and an appetite!

Cusp Dining & Drinks, 7955 La Jolla Shores Dr., La Jolla, CA 92037; (858) 551-3620; cusprestaurant.com; Mediterranean; $$$. At Cusp Dining and Drinks guests especially desire the unforgettable view of the ocean from the 11th floor. The restaurant's beautiful décor is comfortable and never overstated. Enjoy supercharged flavors in a seasonally changing menu where entree-sized portions are called to be shared. The true flavors of every dish shine from locally sourced, seasonal ingredients presented inventively. My favorites include Crispy Pork Belly, Red Snapper Ceviche, Roasted Chicken Breast with Bacon White Wine Caper Sauce, and Roasted Sea Bass with Potato Gnocchi. Another popular item includes a Pan Seared Jumbo Scallop Risotto that surprises guests with a smooth texture and unique curry coupled with grilled oyster mushrooms that lend a delicious smoky flavor. Don't miss the Deconstructed Pavlova for dessert!

Cutwater Spirits, 9750 Distribution Ave., San Diego; CA 92121; (858) 672-3848; cutwaterspirits.com. Born from minds that brought you the immensely-successful Ballast Point Brewery, Cutwater spirits is a novel concept in San Diego. With a vast majority of served spirits made at the in-house 50,000 square foot facility, you'll surely discover some of the best mixed drinks in town. Their top-notch products include Whiskey, Vodka, Gin, Rum, Liqueur and mixers. They even sell some of the most popular mixed drinks in a convenient can! Its massive facility has plenty of space for dining in the window-lined front room, or choose to sit by the spacious bar that's packed during happy hour. Tours of the distillery are also available daily.

Din Tai Fung, 4301 La Jolla Village Drive, #2000, San Diego, CA 92122; (858) 375-5988; dintaifungusa.com; Taiwanese; $$. Traditional Taiwanese fare, specializing in house-made dumplings, wontons and other noodle dishes. This massive dining space is alive with patrons during all hours of operation, and typically requires a lengthy wait to secure a table. Quality product is apparent as soon as you enter the restaurant, with a large glass window showcasing busy workers artistically creating these magnificent signature dishes. A must-have dish is the XiaoLongBao, or Soup Dumplings, accompanied by traditional dipping sauce. A full menu also includes many other Chinese dishes, served hot and steamy at your table.

Draft Republic, Costa Verde Center, 4282 Esplanade Ct, San Diego, CA 92122, (858) 450-1400, cohnrestaurants.com; American; $$. Diners can enjoy innovative American cuisine while choosing from a variety of beers on tap at this popular gastro pub. Don't miss the Draft Republic Burger with half-pound grass-fed beef, American cheese and house-made pickles on a potato roll. Additional location is at 5958 Avenida Encinas, Carlsbad, CA 92008.

Duke's La Jolla, 1216 Prospect St, La Jolla, CA 92037, (858) 454-5888, dukeslajolla.com; Hawaiian; $$$. Duke's La Jolla is a 13,000-square foot restaurant that overlooks the beautiful La Jolla Cove, and features distinct indoor and outdoor dining areas. Guests can celebrate the spirit of aloha with contemporary dishes inspired from Hawaii and Southern California.

Eddie V's Prime Seafood, 1270 Prospect St., La Jolla, CA 92037; (858) 459-5500; eddiev.com; Seafood; $$$. With its expanse of windows, a très chic lounge, and two decks overlooking the La Jolla Cove, this newbie is a strong contender for the city's best view. As for the California cuisine, it's a matter of splurging on top-notch steaks and fresh seafood with a few Asian twists thrown in. A Wine Spectator award-winning wine list doesn't hurt either. Premium hand-cut steaks include a 12-ounce filet mignon embellished with cracked black peppercorns and cognac sauce and an enormous 22–ounce USDA Prime bone-in rib eye that's enough for two to share.

Experience the joined tang and texture in the broiled Pacific swordfish with Jonah crab and avocado, perked up with red chile vinaigrette, or the North Atlantic scallops sautéed with citrus fruits, almonds, and brown butter. The bananas Foster flambéed tableside is the only way to close! Additional location is at 789 West Harbor Drive, San Diego, CA 92101.

Fleming's Prime Steakhouse & Wine Bar, 8970 University Center Ln., San Diego, CA 92122, (858) 535-0078, flemingssteakhouse.com; Steakhouse; $$$. Situated in the Aventine Center across the courtyard from the Hyatt Regency Hotel, think high-end USDA Prime steaks expertly aged a minimum of 21 days, seasoned with kosher salt and black pepper, then broiled at 1600^0 and finished with butter and fresh parsley. Choose from a nice selection of their 100 wines by the glass. Additional location is at 380 K St at, Fourth Ave, San Diego, CA 92101.

Galaxy Taco, 2259 Avenida De La Playa, La Jolla, CA 92037; (858) 228-5655; galaxytaco.com; Mexican; $$. Explore bold Mexican cuisine at this exceptional eatery where they grind their own masa for tortillas daily from heirloom Masienda corn. Tasty Margaritas and specialty cocktails pair perfectly with the made to order guacamole served with all you can eat El Nopalito chips.

George's California Modern, 1250 Prospect St., La Jolla, CA 92037; (858) 454-4244; georgesatthecove.com; California Modern; $$$$. Inundated by locals and visitors wearing everything from tailored suits to designer jeans, an exceptional, unsurpassed flawlessness exists at George's California Modern. An unobstructed ocean view, perfectly placed candles on white tablecloths, impeccable service, and a beautiful wine list are just the start. Earthy and robust dishes include the braised lamb shank with butternut squash risotto, roasted squab, and smoked Maine lobster. Vegetarian offerings prepared at the peak of freshness include rapini-ricotta ravioli or chanterelle stew. Another meatless wonder, the slow-roasted Chino Farm carrot takes on the texture and flavor of fall-off-the-bone braised beef when paired with curried apple puree, glazed turnips, maitaki mushrooms, and toasted buckwheat-brown butter vinaigrette.

Goldfish Point Cafe, 1255 Coast Blvd., La Jolla, CA 92037; (858) 459-7407; goldfishpointcafe.com; American; $$. This café is located uphill from the La Jolla Cove, and the locals like to congregate here for the ocean view and to relax in the classic, yet casual setting. Choose from a large range of specialty drinks including cappuccino, white mocha, hot cider, and Italian soda. A great selection of lighter fare is served for breakfast and lunch. Start your day out right with a veggie burrito or lox and bagel with cream cheese, red onions, capers, and tomatoes. For lunch, choose from a nice selection of salads, specialty sandwiches, and Paninis. I like to order the Bird Rock Sandwich, triple-decked with layers of turkey, ham, bacon, and Swiss cheese. Locals come here for the Panini Milano with pepperoni, salami, melted provolone cheese, and tomatoes on grilled ciabatta bread.

Harumama and Blue Ocean Robata & Sushi, 1250 Prospect St, La Jolla, CA 92037; (858) 999-0323; harumamasd.com; Japanese; $$. Situated above the beautiful La Jolla Cove with expansive ocean views is the dual concept of Harumama and Blue Ocean Robata & Sushi. The 5,783 square foot space is split between the two restaurants, with Harumama in the front and Blue Ocean Sushi appropriately located oceanfront, towards the back of the restaurant. Harumama offers playful takes on Asian fare with inspiration from Chinese, Japanese and Korean cuisines. Seating 58 guests, the restaurant offers the cult favorite and Insta-worthy character steamed buns featuring cartoony pandas, chickens and seasonal characters in flavors like chicken, pork, mushroom and purple sweet potato. Originating in Carlsbad, Blue Ocean Sushi offers an expansive menu featuring items that highlight the fresh flavors of the ocean. Where the Carlsbad location focuses on Robata style cooking, the La Jolla restaurant serves a wide variety of sushi and sashimi. Items that are unique to the La Jolla location include Scallops with black rice risotto, Ribeye Steak, Port Wine Crispy Duck Breast and Campfire Pineapple with beef, shrimp, quail egg, pineapple and vegetables wok-seared in pineapple sauce. Blue Ocean Sushi in La Jolla seats approximately 90 guests.

Harry's Coffee Shop, 7545 Girard Ave, La Jolla, CA 92037; (858) 454-7381; harryscoffeeshop.com; American; $$. The locals know how to situate themselves on a barstool or snuggle with their honey in a booth at this classic old school diner in La Jolla that has stood the test of time since 1961. Early risers grab your coffee and choose from a nice variety of omelets that cause a stir, or batter up with the pancakes and waffles. The famous B.W. Benny or chicken fried steak never disappoints. For lunch the classic Reuben is simply superb!

Herringbone, 7837 Herschel Ave, La Jolla, CA 92037; (858) 459-0221; herringboneeats.com; Seafood; $$$. In the heart of La Jolla and just blocks from the ocean, guests are in for a treat at this beautiful restaurant where dining tables are scattered amongst six live 100-year old olive trees from Napa Valley. As for the menu, Herringbone has a "fish meets field" concept, where the kitchen team takes the freshest ingredients from sea, ranch and farm to create dishes with unexpected flavor profiles based on line-caught seafood and quality meats. The Cold Fare menu is a big hit here! Choose from a variety of local oysters paired with a creative cocktail or opt for the Baja Stone Crab, Big Eye Tuna Carpaccio, Whole Fish Ceviche or Yellowtail.

Himitsu, 1030 Torrey Pines Rd G, La Jolla, CA 92037; 858) 263-4463; himitsusd.com; Japanese; $$$. Inspired by Executive Chef Mitsu, this exceptional prime destination Japanese restaurant specializes in fresh high-quality nigiri, sashimi, sushi and izakaya-style tapas. Ornamented in Asian-inspired décor, the restaurant seats a total of 30 guests, consisting of eight bar seats and 22 patio seats. Mitsu's omakase menu changes nightly, and the sushi bar's inviting aesthetic allow diners an up close and personal opportunity to watch and converse with the chefs. My favorites include the Seaweed Salad, Miso Black Cod, and the Rib-Eye Katsu Sando.

Lemonade, Westfield UTC, 4525 La Jolla Village Dr, San Diego, CA 92122; (858) 251-0912; $$. Enjoy Seasonal California Comfort Food served in a casual, bright cafeteria setting, catering to people looking for a quick lunch or a healthy grab-and-go dinner for the family. The comfortable environment allows for socializing, and also showcases natural design elements including outdoor patios, giant sunflowers and big windows that flood each space with sunshine. Additional location at 3958 Fifth Ave, San Diego, CA 92103

Manhattan of La Jolla, Empress Hotel, 7766 Fay Ave, La Jolla, CA 92037; (858) 459-0700; manhattanoflajolla.com; Italian; $$$. Located inside the Empress Hotel, this elegant Italian-inspired restaurant will put you into a New York state of mind. Celebrities have been known to frequent the restaurant over the years. A delicious menu includes offerings of pasta, seafood specialties, veal, chicken, and steaks and chops.

Mendocino Farms, 8795 Villa La Jolla Dr., La Jolla, CA 92037; (858) 731-8130; mendocinofarms.com; Sandwiches; $$. Located in The Shops at La Jolla Village, this fast-casual gourmet eatery features both indoor and outdoor seating, and a tasty seasonal menu inspired by local produce at an affordable price. Sandwich favorites keep diners coming back for more, especially Chef Judy's Korean Chicken Meatball Sub and the Braised Short Rib and French Onion Melt. Popular salads include the The Sophisticated Chicken and Prosciutto, and the Avocado and Quinoa Superfood Ensalada. Choose from a nice selection of wine, as well as local San Diego craft beer on tap. Extensive and flexible catering options are available daily for pickup and/or delivery. Additional location is at the Del Mar Highlands Town Center at 12873 El Camino Real, San Diego, CA 92130.

©*Maria Desiderata Montana*

Mr. Moto Pizza House, 617 Pearl St, La Jolla, CA 92037; (858) 729-0717; mrmotopizza.com; Pizza; $$. Order a large red pie, a large white, or even a gluten free crust at this local pizza joint. Other classic dishes include calzone or stromboli, and traditional desserts such as New York Cheesecake and Tiramisu. Additional locations throughout San Diego.

NINE-TEN Restaurant & Bar, 910 Prospect St., La Jolla, CA 92037; (858) 964-5400; nine-ten.com; California Modern; $$$$. Escape to NINE-TEN located inside The Grande Colonial Hotel for an unforgettable gastronomic experience! Executive Chef Jason Knibb passionately redefines California cuisine with eloquent presentations and spice-laden touches from his Jamaican background. By gathering veggies and herbs from a garden just outside the back door of the kitchen, Knibb honors his commitment to create innovative cuisine using only the freshest, local ingredients. Treasured dishes include Jamaican Jerk pork belly with spicy jellies and seared duck breast with an 18-year aged balsamic and duck jus. Allow the chef to utterly pamper you, and opt for his "Mercy of the Chef" special prix fixe and wine-pairing menu. Don't miss the warm hazelnut cake with mascarpone cream, figs, balsamic syrup, and Concord grape sorbet.

Pho La Jolla, 3211 Holiday Ct, La Jolla, CA 92037; (858) 587-4688; pholajolla.com; Asian; $. Experience traditional Vietnamese beef rice noodle soup in a savory broth with a choice of meat or veggies. Pho is complimented with fresh mint, cilantro, basil, bean sprouts and sliced chili peppers. If you like it hot and spicy add Sriracha or opt for sweet brown hoisin sauce with a squeeze of lime.

Piatti, 2182 Avenida De La Playa, La Jolla, CA 92037; (858) 454-1589, lajolla.piatti.com; Italian; $$. Nestled in La Jolla Shores, diners can savor Italian fare indoors or dine alfresco on tree-covered patios. Popular menu favorites include the Hot Salami Pizza with house-made Italian sausage, crushed tomato, scallions, oregano and mozzarella or the Saffron Pappardelle with shrimp, tomatoes, garlic, chili flakes, arugula, and lemon and white wine broth.

Pizza Pronto, 7556 Fay Ave, La Jolla, CA 92037; (858) 459-9000, pizzaprontolj.com; Italian; $$. Traditional Italian pizzas are served with a California twist. Choose from a nice selection of homemade sauces, fresh all-natural toppings, and a tangy blend of special Italian cheeses. The crust turns out perfect every time!

Puesto Mexican Street Food, 1026 Wall St., La Jolla, CA 92037; (858) 455-1260; eatpuesto.com; Mexican; $$. Located in downtown La Jolla, this upscale fast-casual eatery features a walk-up counter where you can dine in or get your food to go. The menu offers a variety of authentic Mexican food ingredients including all-natural meats, sustainable seafood, local and seasonally organic vegetables, homemade all-natural stone-ground corn tortillas, and homemade signature salsas made from scratch daily. Customize your guisados (grilled foods), which can be mixed and matched and are served as tacos that are layered with crispy hot cheese. Diners can choose from a variety of toppings such as fish, shrimp, chicken, carne asada, and gourmet Mexican vegetarian items like zucchini flower, corn truffle, and soy chorizo potatoes. For a healthy dessert or refreshing side, Puesto serves a Mexican street cup of sliced jicama, cucumber, carrots, mango, and dried mango sticks with lime, chili, and sea salt. Additional location is at The Headquarters at Seaport, 789 W. Harbor Dr, San Diego, CA 92101.

Rock Bottom, 8980 La Jolla Village Dr, La Jolla, CA, (858) 450-9277, rockbottom.com; American; $$. Discover handcrafted beer at its best with brewers receiving national awards for their unique brewing styles. Upscale bar food is the big draw here, especially the burgers!

Roy's, Costa Verde Center, 8670 Genesee Ave, San Diego, CA 92122, (858) 455-1616; roysrestaurant.com; Seafood; $$$. Located in the heart of La Jolla's bustling business district, experience fusion cuisine at this popular restaurant initially created by Roy Yamaguchi at his original Roy's in Honolulu in 1988. Savor Pacific Rim flavors as you watch the chefs in action in their signature exhibition kitchen!

Seasons 52, Westfield UTC, 4505 La Jolla Village Dr., San Diego, CA 92122; (858) 450-1252; seasons52.com; New American; $$$. Located at Westfield UTC mall, Seasons 52 is a fresh grill and wine bar that provides guests with a healthy dining experience that embraces the living well concept. The menu is inspired by the seasons and the fresh appeal of the farmers' market—52 weeks a year. The food is inspired from many different countries around the world. The chefs start with the freshest ingredients and use natural cooking techniques such as a wood-burning grill to enhance the flavors instead of high-calorie additives. This allows them to keep each menu item under 475 calories, while still maintaining great flavor. Additional location is at 789 W Harbor Dr., #134, San Diego, CA 92101.

Shake Shack, 4309 La Jolla Village Dr #2350, San Diego, CA 92122; (619) 391-1570; shakeshack.com; American; $$. Having earned a cult-like following from around the world, Shake Shack is a modern day "roadside" burger stand known for its 100% all-natural Angus beef burgers and flat-top Vienna beef dogs (no added hormones and no antibiotics ever), 100% all-natural cage-free chicken (no antibiotics ever), spun-fresh frozen custard, and crinkle cut fries. Local brews are available from Latitude 33 Brewing, Ale

Smith Brewing Company, Mission Brewery and Mother Earth Brew Co., plus a rotating seasonal brew from Stone Brewing and Modern Times Beer. In addition to the Shack classics, the Westfield UTC Shack will be spinning up a selection of local frozen custard concretes in a variety of flavors including popular favorites such as Hopscotch and Pie Oh My! Additional location in Mission Valley at 675 Camino De La Reina, San Diego, CA 92108.

Shorehouse Kitchen, 2236 Avenida De La Playa, La Jolla, CA 92037; (858) 459-3300, shorehousekitchen.com; American; $$. Start your day at this popular La Jolla eatery with a cup of freshly ground espresso paired with French toast that's drizzled with 100% pure Vermont Maple Syrup. A menu offering for lunch includes appetizers, soups, salads, sandwiches and Shorehouse favorites. Breads are delivered daily from Bread & Cie Bakery of San Diego.

Shore Rider Bar, 2168 Avenida De La Playa, La Jolla, CA 92037; (858) 412-5308; shoreridersd.com; American; $$. Just steps from the La Jolla Shores, this outdoor eatery offers great food and craft beer, as well as upbeat music in a casual setting. Choose from appetizers, burgers sandwiches, salads, wraps and desserts.

Shores Restaurant, 8110 Camino Del Oro, La Jolla, CA 92037; (858) 456- 0600; theshoresrestaurant.com; California Modern; $$$$. How many places can you step off the sand and immediately into a casual but stylish dining experience? Look no further than The Shores Restaurant, located within a Spanish-style hotel bearing the same name. With a wall of windows right on the beach, you can't find a bad seat in the dining room, lounge, or open-air patio. Serving breakfast, lunch, dinner, and Sunday brunch since they opened in 1970, it's a perfect choice for a family gathering or romantic evening. Each of the menus is extensive and sure to delight even the pickiest of diners. The prix-fixe menu changes regularly, and is offered at a reasonable price, especially when you allow the sommelier to pair your dishes from their extensive wine list. A kids' menu is also available.

Spice & Rice Thai Kitchen, 7734 Girard Ave C, La Jolla, CA 92037; (858) 456-0466; spiceandricethaikitchen.com; Thai; $$. Dine indoors or outdoors and enjoy vegetarian friendly Thai cuisine at this hidden gem in La Jolla. The locals know to come here for the zesty coconut soup, spicy basil noodles, panang curry, and pad Thai.

Sprinkles Cupcakes & Ice Cream, 8855 Villa La Jolla Dr., La Jolla, CA 92037; (858) 457-3800; sprinkles.com; Desserts; $$. I have always been crazy for cupcakes, and Sprinkles in La Jolla is a calming force in my life. Founder Candace Nelson started her cupcake store in Beverly Hills, where customers waited in long lines for these sweet treats handcrafted from the best ingredients. With several locations throughout the United States, Sprinkles has become a household name. From lemon coconut to peanut butter chip, there isn't a flavor you won't find here. My personal favorites are the banana cupcake with bittersweet chocolate frosting and the walnut-studded carrot cake with cinnamon cream cheese frosting.

Sugar and Scribe Bakery, 7660 Fay Ave., La Jolla, CA 92037; (858) 274-1733; sugarandscribe.com; Bakery; $$. Irish classics and French quiche are served at this beautiful La Jolla bakery. Don't miss the Guinness beef stew and vegetarian shepherd's pie. Made from scratch pastries are a hit, especially the assorted tarts and éclairs.

The Cottage, 7702 Fay Ave., La Jolla, CA 92037; (858) 454-8409; cottagelajolla.com; American; $$. Surrounded by boutiques and galleries, this little cottage has it figured out for breakfast, as well as late lunches and dinner. The lines can be long in the mornings, but wait patiently for the fried egg sandwich. This sumptuous concoction of applewood bacon, Gruyere cheese, tomato, arugula, red onion, and lemon aioli all griddled on sourdough bread will make you really happy and full. On the sweeter side, the French toast stuffed with strawberry compote and mascarpone cheese is the perfect pairing with your morning cappuccino. For dinner, it's none other than comfort food therapy with the turkey and Angus ground beef meat loaf with Yukon Gold potatoes and cabernet gravy, or the melt-in-your-mouth polenta cakes with tomatoes, mixed vegetables, goat cheese sauce, and arugula. So much fun food, so little time!

The Marine Room, 2000 Spindrift Dr., San Diego, CA 92037; (858) 459-7222; marineroom.com; French; $$$$. Opened in 1941, this iconic restaurant with its opulent dishes and million-dollar beachfront location continues to attract celebrities, world figures, residents, visitors, and nightly regulars who wouldn't dream of having dinner anywhere else. The seahorse symbol of The Marine Room has long stood for its dramatic on-the-surf location, where waves have been known to crash up against the windows, especially during their popular High Tide breakfast offered on select days during the winter months. Food is magic here, and Executive Chef Bernard Guillas brings an international influence to their cuisine, so much so that they wrote a cookbook called Flying Pans in which they tell of their traveling tales from around the globe with recipes to match. From local seafood favorites to the seasonal and exotic, the menu is an elegant and everlasting tale of two chefs. Soothe your soul with a fennel escargot casserole dressed with white sage gnocchi, pomelo glazed organic tofu with spaghetti squash, or free-range veal osso bucco braised in plum wine.

THE MED, 1132 Prospect St, La Jolla, CA 92037; (858) 818-6887; lavalencia.com; New American; $$$$. La Valencia Hotel, also known as "The Pink Lady," is a Mediterranean style oceanfront resort in beautiful La Jolla, California. Located inside this luxury hotel, THE MED Ocean View Restaurant offers a dramatic dining experience for locals and visitors from all around the world. The menu changes with the seasons and incorporates local, sustainable and organic ingredients for a nice variety of solitary gastronomic preparations. A popular favorite is the Spanish octopus that's poached in white wine with grilled oranges and lemons, ginger, garlic and lemongrass, then vacuum-sealed with preserved lemon. For the grand finale, the octopus is placed on the grill for a quick char then served with a Spanish white bean stew with added chorizo and lobster butter. The signature La V Paella for Two with Bomba Rice, Grilled Seafood, and House Made Chorizo with Shellfish and Chicken is a great choice. There are many other dishes on the menu that make the cut and show real strength in subtle explorations of Mediterranean cuisine. For Dessert don't miss the Italian Panna Cotta with fresh berries.

The Melting Pot, 8980 University Center Ln., San Diego, CA 92112; (858) 638-1700; meltingpot.com; American; $$$. Never fear, fondue is here! After first noticing the romantic and quiet atmosphere, you are taken back to your booth delightfully colored in rich browns and burgundys. In the middle of your table there are burners for where your fondue pot will be placed. Choose from an array of menu items such as the "Traditional Swiss Cheese Fondue" starter, which is a blend of Gruyère and Emmenthaler Swiss cheeses and a splash of white wine as well as some spices for flavor, served with bottomless bread chunks and vegetables. A popular main course is the "Land and Sea," which includes filet mignon, chicken breast, and shrimp. Now, don't be alarmed when a plate of raw meat comes your way. The best part of this whole experience is being able to cook the food in your choice of fondue broth. Delicious sauces accompany the main course, and you will leave feeling satisfied. If you do happen to save room for dessert, make sure to try one of their famous chocolate fondues, which come in many different flavor profiles and are served with sweets including marshmallows, cheesecake bites, and even strawberries and bananas. It's a classy and romantic spot to go for a different, yet memorable dining experience. Additional location is at 901 5th Ave, San Diego, CA 92101.

The Promiscuous Fork, 6984 La Jolla Blvd., La Jolla, CA 92037, (858) 454-3663, thepromiscuousfork.com; American; $$. The locals know this is the place to hang out after a long day of surfing and sun worshipping. A simple menu of fresh ingredients includes offerings of Cajun Dusted Lamb Lollipops that are grilled and topped with a balsamic-hoisin reduction to Asian Braised Short Rib Tacos with ginger slaw, wasabi cream, sriracha and cilantro on a white corn tortilla.

The Public House, 830 Kline St, La Jolla, CA 92037, (858) 551-9210, the-publichouse.com; American; $$. Indulge in Angus and Kobe Wagyu burgers on house made buns with Cajun seasoned shoestring fries. Choose from rotating taps of local San Diego beers, as well as distinctive craft beers and microbrews from all around the world.

We Olive, 1158 Prospect St, La Jolla, CA 92037, (858) 551-8250, weolive.com; American; $$. As well as offering premium California Olive Oils, guests can take in beautiful views of the La Jolla Cove while savoring olive oil inspired dishes and small-production California wines. Guests can also enjoy daily complimentary tastings of all of their California Extra Virgin Olive Oils, vinegars and gourmet foods, while knowledgeable staff members are more then happy to educate and answer questions.

Whisknladle, 1044 Wall St., La Jolla, CA 92039; (858) 551-7575; whisknladle.com; American; $$. In 2008, friends and partners Arturo Kassel and Chef Ryan Johnston established this little neighborhood eatery on the map in La Jolla. The concept was perfect for La Jolla: quaint, cute, modern, and comfortable—you name it! The food is simple, humble, and straightforward with some esoteric choices thrown in. This approach has won acclaim in a number of national and local publications, adding to their positive reputation throughout the culinary community. From flatbread to burgers to charred bone marrow or fried sweetbreads, this made-from-scratch food is fresh, local, and seasonal. One of my favorite starters is the Cutting Board, an assortment of house-cured meats, artisan cheeses, mustards, spreads, and pickles. Another very popular dinner item is the fork-tender braised beef cheek with balsamic cipollini onions, potato puree, and pecorino. Additional locations now include shorter-order items and take-out at the PrepKitchen in La Jolla, Del Mar, and Little Italy.

Ocean Beach, Pacific Beach & Mission Beach

The central beach areas are a vibrant part of San Diego, both day and night. A centerpiece for this cluster of neighborhoods is the Ocean Front Boardwalk, a walkway that runs over 3 miles along the beach from Pacific Beach to Mission Beach, ending at the mouth of Mission Bay in the south. You will find pedestrians, skateboarders, rollerbladers, cyclists, and joggers. A wide variety of shops, bars, coffee houses, and restaurants line the beach, all providing unobstructed views of the wildlife, both in and out of the water.

The beach areas are largely populated by a younger generation, primarily college students, surfers, young professionals, and families. Residences are typically in the form of small cottages, bungalows, single-family homes, and apartment buildings. The nightlife is extremely popular, especially on weekends in the off-season and daily in the summer, when the bars become gathering places for good food, drink, and conversation. Major attractions in the area include Sea World San Diego (opened in 1964) and the historic amusement park Belmont Park in South Mission Beach. Belmont Park was built in 1925 to attract real estate investors and still features the original wooden Giant Dipper Roller Coaster, one of the larger wooden structures of its kind in the US. The park also includes many smaller rides and carnival-type attractions. Adjacent to the boardwalk is Crystal Pier, a public pier and hotel, where you can rent rooms right above the crashing waves.

Across the Mission Bay outlet and right next to Point Loma is Ocean Beach, where the main business activity is along Newport Avenue. Here you will find many restaurants, antiques stores, tattoo and piercing shops, coffee houses, bars, and surf shops. Built in 1966, the Ocean Beach Municipal Pier is the longest concrete pier on the

West Coast, measuring 1,971 feet. The pier, and nearly 1 mile of walkway along the beach, is available to the public for walking and fishing 24 hours a day. In the 1960s, surfing became a critical component of this community, which hosts major surfing events year-round. If you're looking for a fun day at the beach and a simple meal, this is the right place.

Backyard Kitchen & Tap, 832 Garnet Ave., San Diego, CA 92109; (858) 859-2593; backyardpb.com; American; $$. "A Place for PB to Play", this chic and laid back coastal American eatery in Pacific Beach is a natural fit for the seaside neighborhood. A modernly rustic grub-and-brew hotspot, garage doors open to the street inviting all to enjoy interior spaces that are flanked with artfully crafted reclaimed wood interiors. Outdoor areas include three cabanas, fire pits and an indoor/outdoor bar; setting the stage for memorable nights on the patio with late night DJ's and live music. Delicious coastal fare and homemade specialties abound with menus that satisfy hungry appetites for brunch, lunch and dinner.

Bird Rock Coffee Roasters, 5627 La Jolla Boulevard, La Jolla, CA 92037; 619-272-0203; birdrockcoffee.com; Coffee/ Tea; $$. Although technically located in the southern portion of La Jolla, this little coffee shop is really closer to Pacific Beach. Don't let the simple interior and street-front patio fool you; this place has received national recognition for its excellence. Roast Magazine chose Bird Rock as their 2012 winner for Micro Roaster of the Year. Focusing on organic and sustainable beans, they have built strong relationships with their growers, and it's evident in every cup they serve. Their special roasting techniques bring out the best in every bean variety, and the staff is impressive in their attitude and friendliness. Be sure to ask for a cappuccino or latte in a ceramic cup so that you can marvel at the detail used by each barista to ensure your drink is perfectly cupped and marked by an artistic foam leaf. They also offer a small selection of fresh pastries to pair with your perfect cup. No matter what time of the day you visit, you're bound to find locals filling the seats and chatting at this neighborhood-gathering place. Local artists and musicians are frequently featured here. Additional locations throughout San Diego.

Bo-Beau Kitchen + Bar, 4996 West Point Loma Blvd., San Diego, CA 92107; (619) 224-2884; bobeaukitchen.com; French; $$$. Operated by the Cohn Restaurant Group, this attractive and comfortable Ocean Beach bistro celebrates the spirit and flavors of the Mediterranean with a modern yet rustic cuisine. With "Bo" referring to Bohemian style and "Beau" signifying beauty, this newest neighborhood destination offers old-world charm and new-world polish in a French-inspired setting. A most unique feature includes an entrance into the restaurant through an imported ancient Egyptian gate. Adding to the approachability of Bo-Beau is the Mediterranean-inspired cuisine with its wealth of dynamic offerings. Choose from soups, salads, and a variety of house-made pastas as well as house- made pâté and various tartines such as the Croque Madame Tartine, which features a delectable combination of sliced pork belly, gruyere cheese, fried egg, and a Parmesan cheese reduction. The menu also highlights flatbreads adorned with flavorful ingredient medleys ranging from roasted Brie, beets, and curry onion marmalade to braised short rib, horseradish, smashed potatoes, and chives. Additional locations throughout San Diego.

Dirty Bird's, 4656 Mission Blvd., San Diego, CA 92109; (858) 274-2473; dirtybirdsbarandgrill.com; American; $$. Situated in the heart of vibrant Pacific Beach, this newer establishment has a rustic interior filled with wooden furniture and wall accents. Chicken wings are a staple at any bar, but adventurous wings lovers know to come here for the notable hot wings paired with craft beers and sports watching. The menu features 23 wing flavors created with house- made sauces. Crowd favorites include the classic Buffalo, Dirty Ranch, Spicy Garlic, Maple Chipotle and Lemon Pepper. House-made ranch and bleu cheese dips, carrots and celery accompany the saucy delights. Baked low and slow before frying, the wings are juicy, meaty, and, quite honestly, irresistible! There are also plenty of other foods on the menu, including sliders, burgers, salads, and popular tater tots. Where else can you enjoy a plateful of potato rounds loaded with chili and melted cheese? They even offer an ostrich burger, made with naturally low-fat meat and served any way you like. Additional locations throughout San Diego.

Fig Tree Cafe, 5119 Cass St., San Diego, CA 92109; (858) 274-2233; figtreeeatery.com; American; $$. Open for breakfast, lunches, and brunch on Sunday, break your fast in style with a foamy mug of cappuccino and an egg and bacon sandwich with tomatoes, spinach, and mozzarella cheese on toasted brioche bread. The eggs are 100 percent natural from free-range chickens raised on a local family-owned farm in Ramona. The cozy outdoor patio with checkered green tablecloths and potted fig trees appears to be a magnet for neighborhood regulars craving made-to-order food at a reasonable price. For lunch, I recommend chicken breast cordon bleu Panini with smoked ham and bleu cheese on rosemary focaccia bread or the sapphire salad with organic mixed greens topped with turkey, cranberries, goat cheese, and walnuts with lemon-poppy seed dressing. This eatery also welcomes man's best friend, who will love the treats you sneak him under the table! Other locations in Hillcrest and Liberty Station are open for breakfast, lunch, and dinner. Consider their growing catering business for your next special occasion or corporate event, as they offer an extensive menu of hors d'oeuvres and larger menu items. Multiple locations can be found throughout San Diego.

Firehouse American Eatery and Lounge, 722 Grand Ave., San Diego, CA 92109; (858) 274-3100; firehousepb.com; American; $$$. Experience retro-American-chic dining and nightlife experience at this sophisticated, yet approachable restaurant where you can bring the family for breakfast, a business colleague for lunch, or a date for dinner. Standing only a few hundred feet from the beach, this popular hangout is packed year-round, but especially at night when the younger locals are ready to jump-start the evening entertainment. The dining room is cozy but spacious, and the bar is unique, boasting a fiery red hue in the background that makes me feel as if I've entered a fire truck spaceship. An open-air patio and bar upstairs is the best location to enjoy an early morning coffee. Breakfast items include classics like scrambles, waffles, pancakes, and omelets. Their breakfast burrito is especially popular with the locals. Satisfy your craving for something hot and spicy with not one, but three Mini Inferno Burgers topped with pepper jack cheese, grilled jalapeños, and chipotle aioli on sweet Hawaiian bread. And if you're really hungry, opt for the barbecue baby back ribs smothered in Firehouse cider molasses barbecue sauce, and served with fries and slaw on their famous piggy plate.

The Fishery, 5040 Cass St., San Diego, CA 92109; (858) 272-9985; thefishery.com; Seafood; $$. Located in a vintage warehouse just a few blocks from the ocean and in a quieter area of Pacific Beach, the Fishery focuses on products delivered from local artisanal fishermen. Their practices support healthy marine life and sustainability while delivering the freshest seafood available. As such, the menu changes frequently. The daily dinner menu is packed with inspired dishes, like the wild Alaskan Coho salmon miso or macadamia-crusted Alaskan halibut. For a special treat, visit during their "Tuesday Tastings," where you will enjoy a catch straight out of the ocean and prepared with local, organically grown fruits and vegetables. It's a great way to take advantage of the chef's creativity. After your meal, be sure to stroll by the glass cases in the central retail seafood market and choose a fresh catch to prepare at home. The staff is extremely knowledgeable regarding cooking styles that fit the product, so don't be shy! The kitchen also prepares delectable side dishes that complement your meal, always made fresh daily.

Hodad's, 5010 Newport Ave., Ocean Beach, CA 92107; (619) 224- 4623; hodadies.com; Burgers; $$. "No shirt, no shoes, no problem!" Since 1969, Hodad's is a unique, old-fashioned burger joint located in the heart of Ocean Beach just minutes from where the street meets the water. Re-opening in 1991 at their current location, OB residents have been raving about these infamous burgers. With the interior covered in street signs, surfboards, and license plates, it's a great casual place to grab one of the best burgers in town after a long day at the beach. Don't forget the beer either! Served bottled or on tap, there is a great selection of tasty labels to pair with the juicy burger being grilled fresh to order. The all-around favorite here is the bacon cheeseburger, which includes a high-quality ground meat patty, shredded lettuce, pickles, tomatoes, melted cheese, onion, and bacon that's chopped together to almost create another patty. Pair with their onion rings or French fries, and you'll be very satisfied. If you're not in the mood for alcohol, be sure to try their creamy chocolate malt. Although the lines can get long, especially in summer months, it's certainly worth the wait. Multiple locations can be found throughout San Diego.

Isabel's Cantina, 966 Felspar St., San Diego, CA 92109; (858) 272-8400; isabelscantina.com; Latin American; $$$. This place is hip and loud, with festive guests filling seats and having some dining fun for breakfast, lunch, and dinner. Only a few blocks from the ocean, the atmosphere is bright and open by day, transforming to a candlelit haven by nightfall. A gargantuan 15-foot Buddha statue staring down at the dining room and an Asian-style bar in the corner sets the tone for Pan Asian and Latin Fusion cuisine. The menu utilizes fresh ingredients whenever possible, including many that are grown at their own Stargazer Farm, which uses only organic farming practices. From spicy pork carnitas to tofu, you'll savor food with bold and unique flavors created by Isabel Cruz; a self-taught chef who believes that clean, simple, and healthy food can also taste delicious. Test out her theory with offerings such as the soy chorizo tacos, veggie torte, crispy shoestring plantains, or the green chile tamales. Or treat yourself to a special breakfast before heading to the beach, with an extensive list of delicious items. For dessert, the coconut flan is too delicious to pass up!

JRDN at Tower23, 723 Felspar St., Pacific Beach, CA 92109; (858) 270-2323; t23hotel.com; California Modern; $$$$. Enter JRDN at Tower23 Hotel and join the fun at the bar, or take a seat in the sleek and contemporary dining room that includes a massive 70-foot lighted "wave wall" mural. A spacious open-air patio is also the perfect place to enjoy ocean views and watch passersby traveling on the meandering boardwalk. A distinctively modern menu utilizes hand-selected, all-natural meats, the finest seafood from sustainable sources, and locally grown organic produce. It's a perfect brunch destination. Dine alfresco by the ocean and devour Mama's Baked French Toast with sugar and spice pumpkin, whipped mascarpone cheese, and maple syrup. A local favorite is the chilaquiles and eggs, with chorizo, salsa, and queso fresco, avocado, and lime crema. If you dine in the evening, be sure to try one of the fresh catches of the day, or the uber-savory lobster potpie. Open for lunch and dinner daily, brunch on the weekends.

Miss B's Coconut Club, 3704 Mission Blvd., San Diego, CA 92109; (858) 381-0855; missbcoconutclub.com; Caribbean; $$. Tropical birds, tiki gods and colorful flowers come to life in a lively celebration at this Mission Beach restaurant celebrating San Diego's nautical and maritime history. Island-inspired dishes make up for the Coconut Club's unique cuisine, where bold Caribbean flavors meet fruit-infused cocktails, including shareable Tiki-inspired punches and bowls. Feast on Coconut Rum French Toast or a hefty Cuban Roll Sandwich. For a seafood dish unlike any other, try the Jerk Seasoned Jumbo Shrimp with mango chutney and plantain chips.

Pacific Beach Alehouse, 721 Grand Ave, San Diego, CA 92109; (858) 581-2337; pbalehouse.com; American; $$. Enjoy house-brewed beer and craft libations at this world-class microbrewery and restaurant. Nestle into a comfy booth inside for an early dinner, or take in ocean views from the upstairs deck. Sports fans catch your favorite game from one of their 20 new flat screen TV's. Indulge in unique menu offerings, especially their famous Rattlesnake Flatbread with jalapeno, bacon, chorizo and cheeses.

Poma's Italian Deli, 1846 Bacon St., Ocean Beach, CA 92107; (619) 223-3027; pomasdeli.com; Italian; $. Poma's Italian Deli has been a well-known landmark in San Diego since 1965. Tucked away in the heart of Ocean Beach, this joint is easy to miss if you're not on the lookout. I would consider this place a "hole in the wall" deli; however, don't let the lack of decor fool you; the sandwiches have been raved about for years. As you walk in, you notice the cold case in front of the counter packed with fresh lasagna and cold cut meats. Behind that you have choices of beer or wine as well as soft drinks. There is no waiter service; you simply walk up to the counter and order. All of the sandwiches are made there right in front of you, either hot or cold, and are deliciously done on their famous Solunto's bread. Their classic has been the roast beef sub, which consists of hot, tender roast beef chopped up into bite-size bits over their fryer, provolone cheese melted over the top, and then freshly diced tomatoes, shredded lettuce, and whole pepperoncinis. Other famous menu items include the Torpedo sandwich, which consists of cotto and dry salami, mortadella, and provolone, and the simple, yet delicious, meatball with marinara sub. Lasagna, eggplant Parmesan, ravioli, and pizza are also served at this deli. Prices are quite reasonable for the servings you receive.

Red Marlin, 1441 Quivira Road, San Diego, CA 92109; (619) 221- 4868; missionbay.regency.hyatt.com; California Modern; $$$$. Overlooking scenic Mission Bay Marina, choose from a romantic indoor dining room to the outdoor patio directly over the water. They also have private dining rooms and an elegant communal chef's table encircling a built-in fire pit and extensive wine wall. No matter which area you choose, the views are stunning, especially at sunset. As the signature restaurant for the Hyatt Regency Mission Bay, the Red Marlin is open for breakfast, lunch, and dinner, and includes menu selections thoughtfully designed for patrons of all ages. An excellent choice for dinner is the juniper-brined kurobuta pork chop, served with roasted apple, acorn squash, Weiser Farms baby potatoes, and a Dijon demi-glace. Dessert selections change with the seasons, but I will not soon forget my experience with the warm peach shortcake, a heavenly mix of roasted peaches, bourbon sauce, and a pecan biscuit, topped with house-made whipped cream. They also serve a very popular after-dinner drink called the Key Lime Pie, with Absolut Vanilla Vodka, pineapple juice, and fresh squeezed lime.

Sandbar Sports Grill, 718 Ventura Place, San Diego, CA 92109; (858) 488-1274; sandbarsportsgrill.com; American; $$. This two-story eatery has been a popular watering hole and food destination for visitors and the after-work crowd yearning for a relaxed vibe and unfussy food. Since they are open for breakfast, lunch, and dinner, the menu offers hearty omelets, Benedicts, and griddlecakes as well as a simple menu of tapas, burgers, salads, sandwiches, and more. The Sky Bar is the perfect place to watch a sunset and relax with a good draft beer and the popular mahi-mahi fish taco with chipotle aioli and a secret marinade. Crowd pleasers are the crispy natural wings or tenders that come in buffalo style, sriracha garlic, spicy barbecue, sweet chili, or Jose's secret spicy garlic ranch. Bar food that tips the scale includes hand-dipped beer-battered onion rings, cream cheese-stuffed red jalapeños, and carne asada tater tots, but who's counting calories? The Diablo burger may be the best in Mission Beach: a big, juicy patty with chipotle sauce, spicy jelly, fresh jalapeños, pepper Jack cheese, and crispy onions.

South Beach Bar & Grill, 5059 Newport Ave., Ocean Beach, CA 92107; (619) 226-4577; southbeachob.com; American; $$. South Beach Bar & Grill is located right on the corner where palm-lined Newport Avenue intersects with the Pacific. Whether you choose to sit downstairs or on the second-floor bar, your view of the beach activities can't get any better. Since opening in 1992, this eatery in the heart of Ocean Beach has been home to the famous Mahi fish taco. This popular taco delicacy consists of grilled mahi-mahi topped with cheese and drizzled with a generous amount of house-made white sauce and salsa fresca in a soft tortilla. In addition, choose from a variety of fresh seafood as well as great burgers. Grab a seat at the long wooden bar and catch a game from one of the 10 televisions while sipping on a cold brew or specialty cocktail. Their long list of drafts includes a few local craft breweries. Enjoy a dozen fresh oysters on the half shell or clams and green lip mussels steamed in white wine, lemon, and garlic butter.

Sushi Ota, 529 Mission Bay Dr., San Diego, CA 92109; (858) 270-5670; sushiota.com; Japanese; $$$. Unanimously considered the best sushi restaurant south of Los Angeles, this legendary eatery is nearly invisible from the street. Although many lesser competitors try to compensate with flashy exteriors and attractive crowds, Sushi Ota is simply a great place to eat. Every dish is impeccably prepared with the finest ingredients available. The menu is short compared to similar restaurants, because many of the diners pay most of their attention to the fresh menu, which changes daily based on availability. The baked miso salmon and sea bass appetizers are simply amazing. The flavors and textures of every sashimi dish are spectacular. The toro, albacore, and yellowtail are favorites. At times, the room can be extremely crowded, so reservations are a good choice. You'll also need to be a bit aggressive with the sushi chefs, as they are not apt to linger. And don't let the modest location lull you into thinking that the food is cheap. You'll still pay a price for that meal, but it's definitely worth it.

The Mission, 3795 Mission Blvd., San Diego, CA 92109; (858) 488-9060; themissionsd.com; American; $$. So, what can you expect stepping into a bistro named The Mission, strategically located on Mission Boulevard in the Mission Beach neighborhood? Nothing less than artistic and healthy food served in a bright and busy atmosphere. The bistro uses fresh and seasonal ingredients to create simple meals with complex flavors. It is a rare occasion to be seated without waiting. Focusing on giving back to the community, The Mission is regularly involved in local charities, even using the walls to adorn local artist's works. Their sandwiches and many of the breakfasts utilize fresh baked breads from the kitchen. My favorite is the rosemary loaf, crunchy on the outside and soft inside, the subtle flavor of rosemary and olive oil is superb. Or try the fresh cinnamon bread used for their famous French toast. One of the more unique ingredients is the homemade soy chorizo. You would swear it's identical to the meat variety in looks, texture, and taste. My all-time favorite soy chorizo dish is the breakfast burrito, with black beans, crispy rosemary potatoes, scrambled eggs, jack cheese, cilantro, scallions, tomatoes, and chipotle crema in a large whole-wheat tortilla. There are two additional locations in San Diego: downtown in East Village and uptown in North Park.

Tidal, 1404 Vacation Rd., San Diego, CA 92109; (858) 490-6363; paradisepoint.com; California Modern; $$$. Located among the lush surroundings of the Paradise Point Resort, this waterfront restaurant has stunning views of Mission Bay. Choose to sit in the open dining room, near the large and bustling exhibition kitchen, or on the outdoor patio with soft breezes and a warm fire pit. Sunsets are especially popular here, with the crimson light shimmering off the water as sailboats gently crisscross the Bay. Be sure to begin your evening with the French Onion "Bulalo" (bone marrow, shaved truffle, bok Choy and parmesan). For dinner, you can't go wrong no matter what you order. One of the most popular items is the 40-ounce Tomahawk Steak with salsa verde. Be sure to save room for one of the delectable desserts with coffee, and linger to enjoy the night skyline.

Waterbar, 4325 Ocean Blvd, San Diego, CA 92109; (858) 888-4343; waterbarsd.com; American; $$. Perched 20 feet above the bustling Pacific Beach Boardwalk, Waterbar is a spacious and vibrant gathering place, with stunning views of the Crystal Pier and Pacific Ocean. Although the floor plan is quite large for a beach-side location, every square foot is typically filled with patrons enjoying great food, crafted cocktails, and lively conversations. Polished concrete floors, massively high-beamed ceilings and brick walls give it a hip warehouse feel. There's plenty of dining choices throughout the day and into the wee morning hours, including a raw bar, shared plates, full meals, and sweet desserts. Morning Brunch is also served on the weekends. But the big draws are uniquely-imagined cocktails and extensive wine and draft beer selections. One of the more popular libations is a Fish Bowl, with rotating drink recipes served in a large copper pineapple, and certainly meant for sharing!

Old Town, Balboa Park, Mission Valley & Bankers Hill

This section of San Diego is quite diverse, even though the neighborhoods are adjacent to each other in the central part of the county. To really enjoy all of the attractions in this area, you'll need more than one day!

The Old Town area was considered the heart of the city of San Diego until the 1860s, until Alonzo Horton began to develop the downtown and waterfront area. The main attraction for this section of the city is Old Town San Diego State Historic Park, one of the most visited state parks in California. Considering its competition, that's saying quite a lot. Established in 1968, the park commemorates early days of the town of San Diego and includes many historic buildings built between 1820 and 1870. Five original adobes are part of the complex, along with other historic buildings including a schoolhouse, a blacksmith shop, San Diego's first newspaper office, gardens, and a stable with a carriage collection. A number of authentic Mexican restaurants and other quaint eateries are within easy walking distance.

Balboa Park is a 1,200-acre urban cultural park located just north of the downtown area, and attracts over 2 million visitors a year. It was the location of the 1915 Panama–California Exposition and 1935 California Pacific International Exposition, both of which contributed architectural landmarks for future visitors. It was declared a National Historic Landmark in 1977. In addition to open space areas, gardens, and walking paths, it contains a variety of cultural attractions including 16 museums, several theaters, and the world-famous San Diego Zoo. Only one major restaurant is located in the Park, but many others are a short distance away. Bankers Hill is a well-established uptown neighborhood near Balboa Park, and is literally up the hill from downtown San Diego. It includes many restored Victorian mansions, some of which have been modified into offices for dentists, lawyers, and small companies. Although directly under the flight path of aircraft landing at San Diego International Airport, residents are unaffected by the noise. Many popular restaurants are in the area, including both upscale and casual venues, as well as neighborhood delis.

Mission Valley is a wide river valley just north of Old Town, and was the site of the first Spanish settlement in California, established in 1769. This history may be completely lost when you visit the area, as it now serves as a central shopping and entertainment center for San Diego. Three major shopping malls are located here, including Westfield Mission Valley, Fashion Valley, and Hazard Center. The area is also home to a long street known as Hotel Circle, aptly named for the many hotels and motels lining the road. Farther east is Qualcomm Stadium and San Diego State University.

Andres Restaurant, 1235 Morena Blvd., San Diego, CA 92110; (619) 275-4114; andresrestaurantsd.com; Latin American; $$. Since 1983, this small family owned and operated restaurant has a tropical feel complete with fine linen tablecloths, pictures of Cuba on the walls, and Latin American music playing in the background. Although the cuisine is well seasoned, I don't consider it hot and spicy. Choose from beef, chicken, pork, seafood, and vegetarian entrees all served with rice, black beans, and fried plantains. I like the classic Cuban sandwich with roasted pork, baked ham, mustard, pickle, and Swiss cheese. For dinner, I would recommend the Bistec Empanizado, a Cuban-style breaded top sirloin steak, or the Camarones Enchilados, tender shrimp in tomato sauce with onions, garlic, green peppers, and spices. Be sure to stop by their International Latin Market located next door. Here you will find a large selection of hard-to-find spices, food, and non-food items for the serious chef or casual cook. A large banquet room is also available for a special event.

Bankers Hill Bar & Restaurant, 2202 4th Ave., San Diego, CA 92101; (619) 231-0222; bankershillsd.com; California Modern; $$$. Open for dinner only; experience classic and simple New American food at this open and airy contemporary restaurant. Rough wood tables, walls, and beamed ceilings welcome you to a new trend in dining: upscale cuisine that has no item over $20. A rotating seasonal menu offers popular dishes that will excite your senses without emptying your wallet. You'll be surprised to discover deviled eggs as an appetizer, but these aren't your grandma's version: special farmers' market eggs are paired with lemon potato crisps, arugula salad, and Parmesan cheese. Or try the crispy barbecue braised pork tacos, with pepper Jack cheese, avocado, herb-lime cream, and tomato salsa. No matter what you choose, prepare to be astounded. They have plenty of local craft beers available by draft or bottle, and the wine list is equally amazing. Plenty of parking is available nearby.

BUNZ, 475 Hotel Circle S., San Diego, CA 92108; (619) 298-6515; bunzsd.com; American; $$. BUNZ is a casual eatery offering burgers made with Certified Humane Meyer's Natural Angus beef and hormone/antibiotic-free hot dogs. Committed to clean and fair cuisine, Chef-Owner Jeff Rossman uses locally grown produce whenever possible, and even makes his own condiments, including ketchup and beer-thyme mustard. Marvel at a menu that covers breakfast, lunch, and dinner, where no item is over $10. Hands down, the most popular items are in the burger family, and for good reason. The preparations are unique and filled with flavor. Favorites include the Three Li'l Pigs, a burger with smoked bacon, ham, pulled pork, beer-thyme mustard, aged cheddar, lettuce, tomato, grilled onions, and the Cowboy, with smoked bacon, onion rings, house- made beer barbecue sauce, aged cheddar, roasted poblano pepper, lettuce, and tomato. Be sure to ask for extra napkins, because you'll need them to clean up after your culinary rampage. The flattop hot dog preparations are also delicious, with 100 percent premium Angus beef, split down the middle and grilled to crispy perfection. They offer craft beer, wine, and cocktails, but I suggest you savor their strawberry shake or malt, blended to creamy goodness using locally grown berries.

Cafe Coyote, 2461 San Diego Ave., San Diego, CA 92110; (619) 619-291-4695; cafecoyoteoldtown.com; Mexican; $$. Margaritas are flowing and the tortillas are made fresh to order at this Mexican mainstay located in the heart of Old Town San Diego's Historic Walking District. For over 20 years, hungry guests have been satisfying their appetites with hearty Mexican flavors in festive surroundings. The portions for all items are impressive. The super-loaded nachos and a chicken, beef, and potato taquito platter make good communal options, and there are also several seafood choices. The massive beef chimichanga with bell peppers, refried beans, and cheese wrapped in a flour tortilla and deep-fried to give it a crispy golden brown is a favorite as is the Famous Old Town Carnitas, with tender pieces of pork slow-cooked in Mexico's traditional style. Select from over 100 tequilas in the Cafe Coyote Cantina, a certified "Tequila House" by the prestigious Academia del Tequila, Mexico City, and one of only two Tequila Houses in the US. It can get quite busy all day, but the dining room is massive, and typically rotates tables quickly. There are also plenty of shops nearby to keep your attention until your table is ready.

The Cosmopolitan Hotel and Restaurant, 2660 Calhoun Street, San Diego, CA 92110; (619) 297-1874; oldtowncosmopolitan.com; American; $$$. The Cosmopolitan Hotel and Restaurant houses a full-service restaurant and bar, and is the only working hotel in Old Town San Diego State Historic Park. After a $6.5-million rehabilitation and restoration, the place still feels like you've stepped back in time. Imagine tying your horse out front and strolling into a fancy 1800s Western saloon and restaurant. Enjoy both indoor and alfresco dining at surprisingly affordable prices. Of course, the food is much better than what you might have received back in the old days. Creative energy abounds at this eatery where they grow their own fruits and herbs, make recipes from scratch, and serve handcrafted drinks. A few special items are the fennel pollen-dusted Scottish salmon, espresso braised Kobe short rib, and apple-cider glazed Berkshire Pork cheeks. Mexican favorites are still on the menu, including traditional taco and burrito plates, enchiladas, and a root beer brined chicken chile relleno. Don't miss the warm and mouthwatering homemade churros! Open for lunch, dinner, and brunch.

Cucina Urbana, 505 Laurel St., San Diego, CA 92101; (619) 239-2222; cucinaurbana.com; Italian; $$$. This California-inspired Italian restaurant between downtown and Hillcrest has a warm and rustic atmosphere that's a bit understated. The retail wine shop located inside the restaurant allows guests to pick out their own bottles of wine and have them opened at table for a minimal corkage fee. This location is very popular and books up nearly every evening, so reservations are highly recommended. Otherwise, they take first come, first serve walk-ins for the bar, pizza counter, and community table. Ironically, these can be fun options for seating, especially to eat with other people who may just become your best friends. I think what makes this place so popular is great food in good-size portions at an affordable price. The Vasi appetizers are the big hit here, consisting of mini mason jars filled with Tuscan toast and different spreads and cheeses. The pizza and pasta dishes are also big sellers. My favorites are the ricotta gnudi in sage brown butter, the savory short rib pappardelle, or Parmesan panko-crusted eggplant. Its location on Laurel near Balboa Park makes it a perfect destination before or after watching a show at the Old Globe Theater. Their sister restaurant is Cucina Enoteca, located at 2730 Via De La Valle, Del Mar, CA 92014.

El Agave Tequileria, 2304 San Diego Ave., San Diego, CA 92110; (619) 220-0692; elagave.com; Mexican; $$. Tequila lovers know to come here, where a Tequila Museum is home to the largest tequila bottle selection in the US. With over 2,000 brands to choose from, you are sure to find one you like, but don't stop there; taste a few to appreciate the many varieties and subtle differences. The selection can be a bit daunting, so feel free to ask the servers, who are happy to assist and help you find the right blend based on your tastes. The authentic taste of Hispanic-Mexico is served in a beautiful and elegant space, with warm lighting and brick walls adding to the ambiance. Varied spices ranging from chocolate and coriander to garlic and cinnamon make for the fabulous made-from-scratch moles (sauces) used for every dish. I like the Mole Rosa de Taxco, with chicken breast served in a creamy and colorful mole made from walnuts and chipotle chili. Assorted bite-size tamales are also fun, stuffed with shrimp, black beans, and roasted poblano peppers, and topped with a trio of sauces.

El Indio, 3695 India St., San Diego, CA 92103; (619) 299-0333; elindiosandiego.net; Mexican; $$. Founded at the corner of India and Grape as a tortilla factory in August 1940, this was the place to get handmade corn tortillas and the taquito (little taco). In 1947, they moved to the current location, and you can savor the same Sonora-style Mexican dishes that have been served over the years, with no additives preservatives. Tortillas are made fresh every day and are frequently used for care packages sent to soldiers stationed all over the world. It's owned and operated by the same family today, and the menu is so diverse, you'll need to visit more than once to experience the many different dishes. Taquito options include shredded beef, shredded chicken, or potato. Other traditional items include burritos, enchiladas, tostadas, quesadillas, chimichangas, and tamales. One of my favorites is the carne asada nachos deluxe, with plenty of guacamole, sour cream, and beans. Certainly not the lowest-fat option on the menu, but splurging every once in a while, is one of life's pleasures. Be sure to ask for plenty of hot sauce!

Extraordinary Desserts, 2929 5th Ave., San Diego, CA 92103; (619) 294-2132; extraordinarydesserts.com; Desserts; $$. If you are searching for a fabulous dessert location, look no further than Extraordinary Desserts. Owner and Executive Chef Karen Krasne, considered the "Queen of Cakes" according to Gourmet magazine, opened her first Extraordinary Desserts in 1988 on 5th Avenue near Balboa Park. Since then, Extraordinary Desserts has become one of San Diego's most prominent and unique dining establishments and has expanded to include a second location in San Diego's Little Italy neighborhood, as well as a line of gourmet products and a robust online store. She uses organic ingredients whenever practical and possible, and always adorns each luxurious dessert with either locally grown fresh flowers, her signature edible gold leaf, stunning seasonal trimmings, or sinfully sweet sauces. It truly makes her unique creations a feast for the eyes as well as the palate. Krasne's cakes have graced the cover of Bon Appétit magazine, and Forbes recognized her as one of the country's 10 best pastry chefs. She has been featured in the New York Times, Gourmet, Sunset, and the Los Angeles Times, among other publications.

Farmer's Bottega, 860 W Washington St, San Diego, CA 92103; (619) 458-9929; farmersbottega.com; Italain/American; $$. Located in Mission Hills, Farmer's Bottega is a cozy neighborhood eatery offering farm-to-table Modern American-Italian cuisine in a farmhouse setting. The unique decor includes a treadle sewing machine and a 40-year-old tabletop recovered from the ocean. Edison bulbs that dimly glow from iron chandeliers and hallowed wine barrels offer a romantic setting, perfect for that special date night out! Favorite men items include Hearts of Artichoke, Bottega Salad, Swordfish, Heirloom Tomato Flatbread and Flat Iron Pork.

Hob Nob Hill, 2271 1st Ave., San Diego, CA 92101; (619) 239-8176; hobnobhill.com; American; $$. Serving San Diegans since 1944, Hob Nob Hill has been producing breakfast, lunch, and dinner items using the same recipes handed down from the beginning. Nearly everything is prepared on the premises, from the baked items to cured meats. Its popularity has risen to the national stage, as it was featured in the popular Food Network Series Diners, Drive-Ins and Dives, hosted by Guy Fieri. Sit in a comfortable booth by the window, or pick a stool right next to the kitchen. The menu is extensive and covers all of the great American favorites for a very reasonable price. For example, the old-fashioned chicken 'n' dumpling dinner includes your choice of soup or salad, a potato, vegetable, and fresh homemade bread. I have to confess, the chicken-fried steak with extra gravy is a dish that's hard to share with others at your table, so be prepared to defend yourself! The regulars will tell you it's just like Mom's kitchen, and since most modern moms don't cook this way anymore, it may be the best choice for a special meal from yesteryear.

Mister A's, 2550 5th Ave., San Diego, CA 92103; (619) 239-1377; bertrandatmisteras.com; American; $$$$. Located on the 12th floor of the 5th Avenue Financial Center building, experience modern American food with French and Mediterranean influences at this stunning penthouse restaurant just minutes from downtown. The dining room is light and bright with floor-to-ceiling windows boasting panoramic views of San Diego Bay, Balboa Park, Coronado, Point Loma, and even the world-famous San Diego Zoo. Dine alfresco on the heated outdoor patio. A seasonal and revolving menu boasts produce from Chino Farms in Rancho Santa Fe and seafood based on what is available from local purveyors. While French ingredients and techniques dominate, German influences are evident in dishes of spaetzel, choucroute, and house-made sausage. Light and simple preparations that offer a refined elegance include the pan-roasted quail salad with fresh herbs or the medley of shellfish "gratinee" with shrimp, scallops, clams, and mussels in Veloute. The flavorful edge of the cognac- lobster sauce is pure and unabashed in the Maine lobster strudel with forest mushrooms. There is always plenty of delicious butter used in the creation of Mister A's dishes, even if it isn't always mentioned on the menu. Dress code is high-end, so beach attire and baseball caps are not allowed.

New Orleans Creole Cafe, 2476 San Diego Ave., #A, San Diego, CA 92110; (619) 542-1698; neworleanscreolecafesd.com; American; $$. This cozy eatery is located in the Historic Whaley House Gardens in Old Town. The Wild West–style building was built in the 1890s, with a wonderful outdoor patio to enjoy the Southern California weather. Offering authentic Creole dishes based on recipes handed down through 7 generations, many of the ingredients and most   of the beers are imported directly from Louisiana. You will often find the restaurant filled with regular clients who rave about the food and traditional New Orleans–style hospitality. I recommend trying their most genuine dishes: chicken and sausage gumbo, the alligator sausage po'boy, crawfish étouffée, or jambalaya. Each dish is a celebration of the region that will always be known as the Big Easy. And be sure to save room for dessert, because they serve one of the best bread puddings in San Diego.

Old Town Mexican Cafe, 2489 San Diego Avenue, San   Diego, CA 92110; 619-293-3941; oldtownmexcafe.com; Mexican; $$. I've got two words to say about this place: Tuesday. On this special day of the week, you have your choice of chicken, beef, or pork carnitas, fried fish, or potato tacos for a   low price. Tuesday seems to be all the rage, especially with the in-house margaritas, Hornitos shots, and Tecate beer priced at only $2.50. This long-standing Mexican restaurant with three dining areas, an outdoor patio, and traditional-style decorations has been a mainstay for food lovers seeking a fun atmosphere and authentic food options. Aside from the overstuffed tacos, the fajita dishes heaped with beef, chicken, shrimp, or veggies are perfect for sharing. Served with guacamole, half order of beans and tortillas, its more food than you can eat, but do it anyway! Plenty of vegetarian options are also available. They even serve breakfast 7 days a week. Want more excitement? Order the Table Side Shaker Margarita designed to serve two people. Weekend evenings can get packed, so expect a wait.

Saffron Thai, 3731-B India St., San Diego, CA 92101; (619) 574-7737; saffronsandiego.com; Thai; $$. Born in Bangkok, Thailand, to Chinese parents, Chef-Owner Su-Mei Yu opened Saffron Thai Grilled Chicken in 1985 and Saffron Noodles and Saté in 2002 (located right next door). She grew up using cooking techniques handed down from her elders in Thailand, who believed foods have medicinal properties. With this knowledge, Su-Mei Yu made a name for herself with a cuisine specially designed to nourish the mind, body, and soul. The end result is fresh, seasonal, and nutritional fare made on a consistent basis. I recommend the Kung Pao chicken, spicy drunken noodles, and the rad-na wide noodles with beef. All stir- fried noodle and rice dishes can be made with mushroom oyster sauce and/or gluten-free soy sauce upon request for vegetarian and vegan customers. Don't leave without trying the sweet sticky rice with mango for dessert—I might have to eat my dessert first next time! The restaurant is located in a residential neighborhood; so, street parking can sometimes be a challenge.

San Diego Poke Co, 10387 Friars Rd., San Diego, CA 92120; (619) 584-4786; sdpokeco.com; Poke; $$. This popular fast casual restaurant specializes in poke, a traditional Hawaiian dish commonly made with raw ahi tuna. Diners can choose from customizable poke bowls, salads, burgers, wraps, and more. A second store is located at 3533 Adams Ave., in Normal Heights, a neighborhood of the mid-city region of San Diego, CA.

Tahona, 2414 San Diego Ave, San Diego, CA 92110; (619) 255-2090; tahonabar.com; Cocktail Bar; $$. This mezcal bar and tasting room invites guests to feast on a modern Mexican cuisine with Oaxacan flair. Drink offerings include more than 120 varieties of mezcal and creative and classic cocktails crafted by in-house mixologists. A rustic yet refined ambience features authentic Oaxacan elements, oversized Spanish archways leading into the mezcal tasting room, hand painted tiles, Mexican rope seats, large rattan lights and hand troweled clay walls.

The Prado, 1549 El Prado, San Diego, CA 92103; (619) 557-9441; pradobalboa.com; American; $$$. Located in the historic house of hospitality, and across from the Mingei and Railroad Museums, the Prado is a must-see tourist attraction. There is blown glass all around the front entrance, and different patterns are painted along the walls and ceiling. In addition to the central bar and lounge, there are two different eating sections inside. Take your pick from the cozy glass room or spacious courtyard. The heated patio is another nice dining option, where you can enjoy a fantastic view of the lush park-like surroundings. For lunch, choose from great salads, sandwiches, fish tacos, burgers, and soups. The Kobe beef burger and the Kobe beef sushi roll are excellent   afternoon choices. For dinner, there's a little bit of everything ranging from seafood paella or Thai yellow curry chicken and red pepper pappardelle to your basic grilled bone-in rib eye. The dessert menu boasts several decadent delights, sure to complete your meal on the sweet side.

Hillcrest, North Park, South Park & Kensington

This cluster of neighborhoods immediately north of downtown collectively defines Uptown San Diego. It is a densely populated area that has undergone significant revitalization over the years. Tree-lined streets compact blocks, and a walkable business district makes it a popular choice among locals. It is predominantly a single-family residence area with small apartment buildings and bungalows, and is noteworthy for its varied collection of Craftsman and Spanish Colonial Revival style homes built between 1905 and 1930. It is one of the oldest communities in San Diego, and grew tremendously in the early 1900s, thanks to the new streetcar/ trolley system connecting this area to downtown. The Hillcrest neighborhood includes a large sampling of unique restaurants, trendy stores, salons, medical offices, and two major hospitals.

North Park is an architect's dream, with many styles in view, including Craftsman, California Bungalow, Spanish and Mission Revival, Prairie, and Mediterranean. The main business corridor is along 30th Street (north-south) and University Avenue (east- west). Restaurants, coffee shops, bars, and nightclubs are alive with energy at night. Don't look for chain and franchise businesses in this area, as many independents call it home. A number of national magazines have recognized 30th Street as one of the best boulevards to enjoy locally sourced craft beer. Everything is within easy walking distance.

Big Kitchen Café, 3003 Grape St., San Diego, CA 92102; (619) 234-5789; bigkitchencafe.com; American; $$. A bit of trivia here is that Whoopie Goldberg signed a wall in the kitchen here where she used to work alongside Owner Judy Foreman, better known as "The Beauty" On Duty. All trivia aside, you should pay this place a visit for a darn good breakfast at darn good prices! A counter and booths in this diner- type setting makes for great conversation with the staff and other guests. Mainstays on the menu have kept the locals coming back time and time again. Get your share of biscuit and sausage gravy, bacon, bleu cheese, eggs, and mushrooms frittata, tofu rancheros—sautéed veggies and tofu on a corn tortilla with salsa and cheese. They bake their own muffins and coffeecake. They also honey bake their own hams and fresh roast their own turkey breasts.

Bleu Bohème, 4090 Adams Ave., San Diego, CA 92116; (619) 255- 4167; bleuboheme.com; French; $$$. If you're a fiend for French food, this is the place for you! Reminiscent of a French neighborhood bistro with country charm, this blue-tinted Kensington restaurant has a rustic charm all its own. Striving to offer fresh, organic, sustainable, and local ingredients, Chef-Owner Ken Irvine allows the food to speak for itself. Put his Boeuf Bourguignon on your 500-things-to-eat-before-you-die list. This Thunder Ridge Beef simmered in red wine, mushrooms, and smoked bacon is as authentic as it gets. The addition of carrots, baby potatoes, and caramelized pearl onions is so decadent; it's easy to forget you're eating your vegetables. And every bit of sauce begs to be sopped up with a crusty French bread—yes, it's that good! If that entire flavor isn't enough for you, ask for the melted Camembert Fondue cheese in a box. With a pleasant kick of Calvados brandy, sliced apple, and baguette croutons, it'll knock you for a loop—in a good way!

Buona Forchetta, 3001 Beech St, San Diego, CA 92102; (619) 381-4844; buonaforchettasd.com; Pizza; $$. Located in the South Park neighborhood of San Diego, Buona Forchetta serves hungry diners what may very well be the best Napoleon-style pizzas around, as well as antipasti, insalate, specialty pastas, meat and seafood dishes, and delicious house-made dolci. This popular pizzeria is the talk of the town with its large, hand-made pizza oven (named Sofia and built on-site by Stefano Ferrara), taking center stage in the kitchen. Popular pizza favorites include the Puttanesca with mozzarella, capers, anchovies and olives or the Marinara with oregano, garlic and grape tomatoes. In addition, all pizzas can be made gluten-free. I highly recommend the Housemade Beef and Pork Meatballs with tomato sauce and Parmesan, the Polenta with Mushrooms in Wild Boar Stew or the traditional Ossobuco Alla Milanese. The beer and wine menu showcases a nice variety of craft and small-production labels from California and Italy, as well as classic house made red or white Sangria.

Bread & Cie, 350 University Ave., San Diego, CA 92103; (619) 683-9322; breadandcie.com; Bakery; $$. Established over two decades ago, Bread & Cie was the first artisan bread bakery in San Diego. As a testament to their high-quality product, they are now baking daily for over 150 dining and shopping venues in the county, and offer bread and pastries to restaurants, markets, caterers, and hotels. It's hard to resist the luscious pastries and fresh- baked bread aroma that this specialty bakery provides. For breakfast, sip on a tall cappuccino paired with a cream cheese Danish, or the decadent French toast Panini stuffed with mascarpone fruit compote. Soups, salads, and specialty sandwiches are available for lunch. My husband's fave is the roasted portobello mushroom sandwich served on rosemary-olive oil bread, packed with portobellos, zucchini, onions, and Parmesan cheese.

Cafe 21, 2736 Adams Ave., San Diego, CA 92116; (619) 640-2121; cafe-21.com; American; $$. Owners Alex and Leyla, from Baku, Azerbaijan, have put their heart and soul into this diminutive eatery in Hillcrest. Don't be fooled by the worn-down exterior and neighboring businesses, as you'll be pleasantly surprised when passing through the front door. Significant work has led to a modernized interior that provides an upbeat atmosphere. Regulars come here to savor exotic and flavorful foods, as well as attentive staff willing to converse about any subject. The menu is considered "New American cuisine" and includes signature homemade flatbread sandwiches, fresh organic salads, hearty breakfasts, and a wide selection of coffees, teas, wine, and beer. I like to come here for breakfast to enjoy their rendition of French toast "Azeri style," stuffed with a mascarpone and ricotta cream cheese filling. It makes a perfect pair with one of their robust coffees or wide selection of organic teas. For dinner, choose the Azerbaijani-style kabob platter with house-made lamb sausage, Azeri seasoned chicken, and beef kabobs served over curry almond basmati rice pilaf with their special house dip and pickled vegetables. Other popular items are the stuffed cabbage rolls and rosemary trout. Space is limited, so you may need to wait on the busier mornings or evenings. Additional location is at 802 Fifth Ave, San Diego, CA 92101.

Cafe Bassam, 3088 5th Ave., San Diego, CA 92103; (619) 557-0173; cafe-bassam.cafes-city.com; Coffee/Tea; $$. Since 1991, Cafe Bassam has been a well-known wine and tearoom as well as coffee bar. As you walk in, you first notice the atmosphere and decor, which is very old-fashioned. Many antiques to look at and very rustic; you almost feel like you are taking a peek into the 1920s era. There are chairs with tables and a couch to lounge on while you drink a large beverage of your choice. Secondly, you see the pastry case filled with delicious sweets that are paired very well with any drink you choose. Located on 5th Avenue and nestled away in Hillcrest San Diego, it's the perfect place to grab a hot drink or a decadent pastry and socialize while being in the city. Ordering the raved-about chai latte, the first thing you'll notice is how huge the cup is. The chai is foaming and delicate tasting, not too sweet yet not over powerful with flavor. Other favorites are their dark hot chocolate as well as their very wide range of teas that they provide. Come here for a great, dimly lit atmosphere that's perfect for a pit stop on the way to a movie or somewhere to just simply relax.

Caffé Calabria, 3933 30th St., San Diego, CA 92104; (619) 291-1759; caffecalabria.com; Italian; $$. Founder Arne Holt has made his dream a reality. Proud to roast the finest coffee on-site for his patrons, the aromas as you enter the door are unmistakable. Coffee is roasted in small batches on-site at this comfortable cafe centrally located in North Park. From espresso extraction to milk texturing, skilled baristas are busy over buzzing espresso machines making you the perfect cup of Joe. One taste of my cappuccino convinced me that I would never buy beans in a grocery store ever again.

Chocolat Bistro—Creperie—Cremerie, 3896 5th Ave., San Diego, CA 92103; (619) 574-8500; chocolat-hillcrest.com; Desserts; $$. Born in Milan, Italy, with its debut American location in San Diego, Chocolat entices patrons with authentic Italian gelato, warm and delicious homemade crepes, wood-fire pizza, handmade pastas, and Paninis. Alessandro Minutella, the founder of the US Chocolat concept, showcases authentic recipes and time-honored traditions of Italy's gelato and pastry artistry. Two dozen gelato flavors made from top- of-the-line ingredients include amaretto chocolate, nutellone, honey and poppy seed cream, and fruit flavors like mango, lemon strawberry, wild strawberry, basil lemon, and chocolate pear. Available daily, a new all-day brunch features a wide variety of offerings, including sticky macadamia and apples, consisting of grilled panettone stuffed with baked apples, honey, macadamia nuts, and mini marshmallows. There is an additional location in the heart of the Gaslamp Quarter.

Eclipse Chocolat, 2145 Fern St., San Diego, CA 92104; (619) 578-2984; eclipsechocolat.com; Desserts; $$. Driven by high standards, Eclipse is a special company with exquisite products. Just read their mission statement: "to provide premium artisan foods & confections with a unique culinary perspective while maintaining sustainable & ethical operations and contributing to our local community." They source all of their chocolate from the famed Guittard Chocolate of San Francisco, a family-owned company in business for 150 years. Quality and sustainability are paramount, as the company does its part to give back to the farmers and environment. In addition to being avid recyclers, they only use corn-based and post-consumer paper products for their consumer containers. They pride themselves in preparing and packaging all of their products by hand. Entering their small cafe is an experience akin to a child's dream. Enjoy a variety of drinking chocolates, dessert trays, and espresso drinks. Their most popular items are the crème fraiche cupcakes in 24 different flavors with either dark chocolate or vanilla butter cake, a special filling, and chocolate ganache glaze. Once a month they also offer a full-service three-course tasting dinner that incorporates chocolate, vanilla bean, or caramel in each plating. Wine and beer are available to pair with your dishes. Be sure to reserve a table in advance. Many of their products are available online or at exclusive retail stores in several states.

Empanada Kitchen, 2855 El Cajon Blvd., Suite 3, San Diego, CA 92104; (619) 228-9565; empanada-kitchen.com; Argentine; $. This casual restaurant originated at the North Park Farmer's Market in 2016, and its first brick and mortar location opened in February 2018 in Downtown San Diego. After less than one year Downtown, Empanada Kitchen was named one of "Yelp's Top 100 Places to Eat in the U.S. 2019." This accolade, along with much additional praise and demand for their golden-brown baked empanadas, motivated an expansion with a new location in one of San Diego's favorite boroughs. Empanada Kitchen North Park is located at serves quality handmade and authentic Argentine empanadas. Stemming from the Spanish word "empanar," which means to fold or wrap in bread, empanadas are a staple cuisine in Argentina; each region of the country having its own style and manner of preparation. A variety of empanada flavors are available including vegetarian and vegan options, as well as seasonal savory and sweet ingredients. Savory empanadas are always accompanied with homemade chimichurri sauce made fresh every day following a traditional gaucho-approved recipe. Empanada Kitchen Downtown is located at 819 C Street. San Diego, CA 92101.

Et Voilà! French Bistro, 3015 Adams Ave, San Diego, CA 92116; (619) 209-7759; etvoilabistro.com; French; $$$. This cozy restaurant offers a romantic and relaxed atmosphere for couples, families and friends. The extensive menu is replete with both traditional and contemporary French dishes. The duck confit, coq au vin, steak tartare, onion soup gratinee, moules frites, and escargot are some of their most popular dishes. Don't forget about dessert! You will regret leaving before you try the soufflé.

Fort Oak, 1011 Fort Stockton Dr, San Diego, CA 92103; (619) 722-3398; fortoaksd.com; New American; $$$. Fort Oak features New American cuisine with a subtle French influence. Think farm-to-table and forest-to-table with a seasonal selection of small plates and composed dishes cooked over an open flame, offering live fire flavor. The menu consists of organic, local and sustainable ingredients and produce. The house plate selection includes anything from Coppa Ham with B&B pickles, to Salami with cabecou cheese or Rabbit Sausage with apricot mostarda. For a truly memorable dining experience, take a seat at the chefs counter (we did), where you can watch all the action take place in an open kitchen.

Hash House A Go Go, 3628 5th Ave., San Diego, CA 92103; (619) 298-4646; hashhouseagogo.com; American; $$$. Bar none, this is one of the best places to come if you are really hungry and love gigantic-size portions of twisted farm food with a Southwestern flare. I hate to sound redundant, but it's basically comfort food with a twist. The inside of this restaurant is a great place to watch everything go down. They play really loud music, including rock and roll, and the tables are really close together. Large portions are served on surfboard plates and are easily sharable. Farm Benedicts with homemade sauces of chipotle, chili, and barbecue cream are popular for breakfast. Your mama's fried chicken is now Andy's Sage Fried Chicken with a bacon waffle tower drizzled with hot maple reduction and fried leeks. They are well known for their Bloody Mary's made with their own house-made spices. Reservations are recommended especially for large groups.

La Catrina Tapas & Cantina, 3139 University Ave, San Diego, CA 92104; (619) 436-0060; lacatrinacantinasd.com; Mexican; $$. Transporting distinct flavors and style across the border, this modern-casual bistro, with its vibrant surroundings and flamboyant accents, offers a Baja-inspired menu of colorful Mexican tapas, wine, beer and more. Patio seating is available along with high-top bar spots and community tables for sipping and savoring each selection.

Louisiana Purchase, 2305 University Avenue, San Diego CA 92104; (619) 228-9990; louisianapurchasesd.com; Cajun/Creole; $$$. Get a taste of authentic New Orleans-style food and cocktails at this intimate establishment boasting a modern interpretation of a classic French Quarter restaurant. A rotating menu features the big and bold flavors of the South, including Andouille Fried Red Beans and Rice, Fried Redfish, and savory Alligator Cheesecake. A must-visit cocktail bar focuses on quality and craftsmanship, with modern plays on classics like the Ramos gin fizz and the Sazerac, in addition to sharable punches.

Medina Moroccan Baja Kitchen, 2850 El Cajon Blvd., Suite #4, San Diego, CA 92014; (619) 230-5037; medinakitchen.com; Moroccan; $$. Located on El Cajon Boulevard in North Park, this fast-casual eatery boasts a modern and colorful design while offering fresh Moroccan food with Baja California-inspired flavors and ingredients. Enjoy lunch or dinner with local craft beers and a selection of eclectic wines, including varietals sourced from Mexico's Valle de Guadalupe wine country. Outdoor seating with soothing azure blue and white tiles is reminiscent of lounging by the Mediterranean Sea.

Muzita, 4651 Park Blvd., San Diego, CA 92116; (619) 546-7900; muzita.com; African; $$$. Sharing a traditional Abyssinian (Eritrean/Ethiopian) meal with family and friends at this hospitable neighborhood hideaway in University Heights is nothing short of a tasty adventure. When you enter, you can immediately smell the aroma of spices and homemade cooking coming from the kitchen. Dine inside or on the cozy outdoor patio while listening to African music and discussing the East African decor. Since Owner Abel Woldemichael is from Eritrea, a country in northeast Africa, he offers authentic family recipes reminiscent of the old country. A knowledgeable wait staff will guide you through the menu. Most of the dishes contain exotic spices such as cardamom, coriander, and cloves. Diners can opt to share large platters of food, served family style. Don't worry about reaching for a fork; use your hands and eat the food the traditional way. An Ethiopian staple, the injera bread is made from a grain called "teff" (one of the smallest grains in the world). It has a spongy, pancake-like texture, and guests tear off the bread, one piece at a time, to scoop up the food. One of the most popular dishes with the guests is the kitfo. It is raw (or rare) hand-minced beef with marinade rub in mitmita (a spicy seasoning).

Nomad Donuts, 3102 University Ave, San Diego, CA 92104; (619) 431-5000; nomaddonuts.com; Donut Shop; $. Nomad Donuts is a place that makes you think outside the box when it comes to your not so ordinary donuts. In fact, these eclectic and artisanal donuts prove to be downright dreamy (even the vegan ones), specially handcrafted from small batch ingredients chosen from farmers markets, including cage free, organic eggs from local farmers. The 50-donut menu changes daily and often reflects seasonal themes with flavor combinations that range from the exotic to the unusual, with recipes that have even inspired a few limited-edition craft beers. Start your day with a hot 'Pooh Bear' latte and a delicious Mexican hot chocolate horchata donut!

Parkhouse Eatery, 4574 Park Blvd., San Diego, CA 92116; (619) 295-7275; parkhouseeatery.com; American; $$$. Parkhouse Eatery is a laid-back, yet well-designed neighborhood eatery closely nestled into the house that once held the St. Vincent de Paul thrift store. Dining options include an outdoor garden patio, a window-lit living room, and what the locals refer to as a comfy and cozy "hearth room" with a wood-burning fireplace. Incorporating free-range eggs and mostly organic vegetables, its back to the comfort food basics with generous portions of fancy scrambles and blue cornmeal flapjacks offered for breakfast. Well-executed lunch specialties include delicious salads, sandwiches, and entrees. I recommend the griddled turkey meat loaf sandwich with hand-cut russet French fries with homemade chunky ketchup. Straightforward dinner options include steaks, seafood, poultry, and lamb as well as pizza and pastas. The popular five-mushroom polenta cake surpasses all expectations!

Sabuku Sushi, 3027 Adams Ave., San Diego, CA 92116; 619-281-9700; sabukusushi.com; Japanese; $$$. Nestled in Normal Heights, this contemporary neighborhood sushi bar continues to surprise diners with time-honored sushi rolls and a unique blend of Japanese cuisine with an American flare. In addition to classic nigiri, sashimi, and rolls, fresh and unique ingredients exhibit a wide range of flavors. Two standout examples are the Bacon and Scallop Roll, and the signature Chillaxin Roll, made with shrimp tempura, spicy crab, a spicy ginger aioli glaze, and baked Chilean sea bass. In addition, Sabuku Sushi makes it a point to carry traditional filtered and unfiltered sakes, along with flavor-infused versions with hints of plum, Asian pear, and coconut lemongrass. Even the cocktails are infused with sake, like the Mimosa Ke, a combination of sparkling sake and orange juice. Visually, Sabuku Sushi takes a minimalist approach with a modern atmosphere designed to calm and soothe. Sleek metal accents, dark wood tables, and large windows provide a panoramic view of the street and allow natural light to flood the space.

Tajima Ramen Bar, 3739 Sixth Ave, San Diego, CA 92103; (619) 269-5050; tajimasandiego.com; Japanese; $. It's all about made from scratch ramen and a menu that honors the purity of Japanese taste and style. Enjoy dining at Tajima's tastefully decorated restaurants, which offer community tables and private seating areas, along with artful décor and lighting. Tajima offers one of the widest selections of Japanese cuisine available at affordable prices. Sourcing the freshest ingredients available, the daily tapas-style (small plate) menu changes with the seasons. Multiple locations throughout San Diego.

Taste of Thai, 527 University Ave., San Diego, CA 92103; (619) 291-7525; tasteofthaisandiego.com; Thai; $$$. Opened as one of the first vegetarian restaurants in San Diego, Taste of Thai was instantly home in the eclectic Uptown area. Established when Thai cuisine in Southern California was still in the fledgling stages, its popularity has increased significantly, resulting in numerous awards nearly every year. With a bright and elegant dining room, you'll find the service prompt and courteous. However, it can be very crowded on any given day, and for good reason. Locals are in love with cuisine that is fresh, spicy, and full of flavor. You'll notice the quality and freshness of ingredients in every dish. Their fresh spring rolls are a perfect example. Light-as-air rice paper is stuffed with lettuce, bean sprouts, mint, vermicelli noodles, and shrimp (or tofu) and served with a special house sauce. Two of my favorite entrees are the vegetarian/tofu hot basil, with green pepper, onion, chili, and garlic; and the spicy duck, a half duck topped with green pepper and green beans, served in a sweet and spicy curry sauce. After all of that delicious spicy food, don't forget to order the classic fried banana and ice cream. A perfect ending to the meal! Additional location is at 15770 San Andres Dr., Del Mar, CA 92014.

The Smoking Goat, 3408 30th St., San Diego, CA 92104; (619) 955-5295; thesmokinggoatrestaurant.com; French; $$$. Small in stature and surrounded by plenty of choices in the North Park area, this cute bistro stands tall. Trendy artwork adorns the walls, and soft lighting helps set the mood. Serving what they call "French & American countryside fare," the meals are made from fresh, simple ingredients, but prepared with modern influences. No matter what you order, be prepared to enjoy the highest quality meats and produce. The local organic beet salad and butternut squash ravioli that I enjoyed one night were tremendous. There are usually a few uncommon meat dishes available for the adventurous. The wine and beer list changes regularly and include some interesting labels worth trying.

TRUST Restaurant, 3752 Park Blvd, San Diego, CA 92103; (619) 795-6901; trustrestaurantsd.com; New American; $$$. If you're looking for a unique farm to table experience in a high-energy atmosphere where people are eating and talking loudly over ingenious food and drink, then the newly opened TRUST Restaurant in Hillcrest is the place for you. The décor is simple, yet stylish, featuring a communal bar and American White Oak dining tables and chairs. It's the kind of place where you will gain a greater appreciation for the culinary craft. Watch the chefs in action, cooking as a team in their element, plating delicious presentations and grabbing mason jars filled with pickled fruits and vegetables off the shelf.

Underbelly North Park, 3000 Upas St., San Diego, CA 92104; (619) 487-9909; godblessunderbelly.com; Asian Fusion, Ramen; $$. Bring your appetite to this sleek and unique eatery that offers seating indoors, as well as open air seating outdoors where a gas 'Rubens tube' dancing fire feature moves to the beat of the music overhead. Explore a rotating ramen menu with options ranging from beef brisket, teriyaki chicken, and bacon wrapped mushrooms to eggplant wrapped tofu and chasu belly. A popular favorite is the Belly of the Beast Ramen with soft-boiled egg, oxtail dumplings, beef brisket and hoisin glazed short rib. Don't miss the Pork Belly Buns with pickled cucumber and ginger hoisin mayo. Yakitori selections include bacon wrapped asparagus, pork belly, sirloin, and shisito peppers. Rice Bowls of fried or brown rice are available in meat or vegetarian options. Choose from a great list of local brews as well as wine and sake. Underbelly's sister space is located at 750 W. Fir St, #101, San Diego, CA 92101.

URBN Coal Fired Pizza, 3085 University Ave., San Diego, CA 92104; (619) 255-7300; urbnnorthpark.com; Pizza; $$$. Joe Mangini opened the doors to URBN Coal Fired Pizza in Vista in 2008 and, most recently, a second location in the progressive North Park neighborhood. Taking up a 5,000-square-foot space, this restaurant specializes in coal-fired thin-crust pizzas, local craft beers, Italian wines, and a selection of fine tequilas. The pizzas come with toppings you've most likely never eaten before. White pies are topped with anything from fresh clams and Parmesan cheese to mashed potato and pancetta. I also love the red pies, especially one topped with gorgonzola-stuffed cherry peppers and fresh mozzarella or the meatball pie with sautéed red onion and ricotta. Of course, the coal-fired wings aren't too shabby either! Multiple locations can be found throughout San Diego.

Coronado, Harbor Island, Shelter Island & Point Loma

Although not technically part of the downtown core, this cluster of coastal communities resides in a unique area between the Pacific Ocean and San Diego Bay.

Harbor Island and Shelter Island are located on the north and west sides of San Diego Bay. These man-made peninsulas are lined with marinas, hotels, restaurants, and an exclusive yacht club. Views from every possible location are absolutely stunning, looking across the bay at downtown San Diego. Situated between the centrally located International Airport (Lindberg Field) and the Coronado Naval Air Station, you're bound to see (and hear) a variety of aircraft zooming overhead. This is an amazing opportunity to sample upscale cuisine on the waterfront. Don't be surprised to see boaters mooring at specially designed landings right next to your balcony table. Daily charter fishing boats are also available, if you're interested in catching your own dinner.

At the most western end of the bay is the long, hilly peninsula of Point Loma, which is sandwiched between the bay and Pacific Ocean. Often described as "where California began," this area was discovered by the first European expedition to land in 1542. Don't miss the Cabrillo National Monument and Old Point Loma Lighthouse at the very southern tip. Liberty Station is a modern retail and commercial center built on the site of the former Naval Training Center. Several excellent restaurants are located in this area as well as a large waterfront park.

Located on a small peninsula directly across the bay from downtown is Coronado, an oasis that can be accessed via the landmark Coronado Bridge, or along the thin isthmus dubbed the Silver Strand that leads to the South County area. This is one of the most expensive places to live in the US, and for good reason. No matter where you reside in this town, you're within walking distance of the Pacific Ocean as well as San Diego Bay. When the legendary Hotel del Coronado opened in 1888, this town officially became a major resort destination. Orange Avenue is the main street through the town and is lined with restaurants, shops, theaters, and hotels. For a real treat, take the ferry between downtown San Diego and Coronado, where you can easily travel by foot (or bike) to all of the major attractions.

Bali Hai, 2230 Shelter Island Dr., San Diego, CA 92106; (619) 222-1181; balihairestaurant.com; California Modern/Asian Fusion; $$$. Located on the northern tip of Shelter Island, Bali Hai was opened in 1955 by San Diego restaurateur Tom Ham. It's been family owned and operated for over five decades. It was the island's first "tiki temple," named after the song popularized by the musical South Pacific. Two famous tiki icons were created for the structure: Mr. Bali Hai, a large wood sculpture at the front entrance greeting guests, and The Goof, a playful and mysterious remnant that has stood guard on the restaurant roof for over five decades. This iconic Shelter Island dining spot—known for its sweeping bay front views, oversized Mai Tais and distinctive Pacific Rim cuisine—boasts approachable fresh flavors. Don't miss the coconut curry steamed mussels, blackened albacore, char siu glazed duck, and Kalua pork tenderloin.

Cesarina, 4161 Voltaire St, San Diego, CA 92107; (619) 653-3264; cesarinapasta.com; (619) 653-3264; Italian; $$$. Cesarina is a lively Italian trattoria situated in the heart of Point Loma's upper Voltaire Street corridor. Enjoy all-day dining with a nod to European-style breakfast. The open-air 'pastificio' (pasta factory) is visible for all to see while churning out fresh handmade pasta daily. Drawing upon traditions of rustic Italian cooking, the restaurant is also an advocate for locally grown produce and sustainable farming practices.

City Tacos, 805 Seacoast Dr., Imperial Beach, CA 91932; (619) 621-5814; imperialbeachstreettacos.com; Mexican; $. Just steps from the sand, this local beachside hangout offers traditional street and seafood tacos with a Southern California flare. Pair your bites with a Mexican soda or daily made Agua Fresca. Both indoor and outdoor seating is available. Multiple locations can be found throughout San Diego.

Coasterra, 880 Harbor Island Dr, San Diego, CA 92101; (619) 814-1300; cohnrestaurants.com/coasterra; Mexican; $$$. This 28,000 square-foot bayfront modern Mexican restaurant, lounge, and event space on Harbor Island offers a compelling combination of panoramic views of San Diego's downtown skyline. The menu features regional Mexican cuisine with a focus on unexpected flavor combinations, with an emphasis on local, fresh, seasonal ingredients. More than 70 labels of agave spirits including high-end tequila and artisanal mezcal is yours for the asking. Guest can also choose from a robust wine list, including Latin America and Baja varietals, as well as sixteen local and Mexican craft beers on tap.

Con Pane Rustic Breads and Cafe, 2750 Dewey Rd., San Diego, CA 92106; (619) 224-4344; libertystation.com; Bakery; $$. With a spacious location in the ever-expanding Liberty Station area, this bustling bistro is truly carb heaven! Owner Catherine Perez says that the word "companion" derives from con pane (with bread), and this is the perfect choice for enjoying a meal with friends or family. This bakery offers several tables by sunny windows, a large patio area, and an endless variety of freshly baked bread to enjoy. The popularity of this establishment can be measured by the typically long lines of patrons waiting to order their favorite breakfast or lunch. Everything is made from scratch, with a menu offering over 20 flavors of handmade artisan breads, decadent morning pastries, inventive sandwiches, and aromatic coffee and espresso drinks. The savory loaves are by far the most popular item and include favorites such as rosemary olive oil, kalamata olive, Gorgonzola, and roasted red onion. So, pull up a chair, order a big mug of foamy cappuccino and one (or two) of the now-famous cinnamon rolls, and enjoy a break from the hectic day!

Corvette Diner, 2965 Historic Decatur Rd., San Diego, CA 92106; (619) 542-1476; cohnrestaurants.com; American; $$. If you're looking for a quiet, romantic evening, this is certainly not the place to visit! But I have to admit; it's one of my secret indulgences when I am craving good, 1950s diner food with plenty of free entertainment. Lots of chrome, flashing lights, waitresses with bouffant hairdos and poodle skirts, and plenty of singing and laughing. This destination is as much about the atmosphere as the food. My recommendation? Go for the chocolate-peanut butter banana malt and Dante's Inferno Burger, with jalapeño mayo, pepper jack cheese, lettuce, tomato, onion, and jalapeños. Another option is to forget dinner and just order the gigantic brownie hot fudge sundae or banana split boat. Either one will blow your calorie count for the week, but what a way to go! This is definitely a great spot for families, especially during a birthday celebration.

Crown Landing, 4000 Coronado Bay Road, San Diego, CA 92118; 619-424-4000; crownlanding.com; American; $$$. Boasting a nautical theme, Crown Landing is a must-see restaurant located inside the beautiful Loews Coronado Bay Resort, a destination hotel that draws both national and international travelers alike. An onsite chef's garden is coupled with fresh farmer's market produce to keep the seasonal menu in check. Try the Butternut Squash Bisque with chive purée or the Dungeness Crab Cake with avocado, cucumber, and lime ginger dressing. Other favorites include Shrimp Toast with Napa cabbage slaw, candied jalapeños, and sesame seed aioli, or the Cavatelli Pasta with calamari, spiced fennel sausage, and fennel purée. Who doesn't love a Lobster Boil? They have a good one here!

Cupcakes Squared, 3772 Voltaire St., San Diego, CA 92107; (619) 226-3485; cupcakessquared.com; Desserts; $. Owner Robin Wisotsky offers one-of-a-kind "square" gourmet cupcakes made from top-of-the-line, natural ingredients including Cacao Barry chocolate and fresh Hawaiian vanilla shipped in weekly. No preservatives or stabilizers in these delicious cakes. Wisotsky even grinds fresh almonds to make almond flour. Cupcakes are baked from scratch fresh daily and come in over 28 flavors. My faves are the Not So Red Velvet with mild cocoa and vanilla cake with cream cheese frosting, the pistachio cake with pomegranate butter cream, and the Mocha Baileys with rich chocolate and coffee flavors and Bailey's Irish cream frosting. Most cupcake flavors can be ordered gluten free and a baker's choice of gluten-free cupcakes is available every day!

Devine Pastabilities, 3545 Midway Dr., #E, San Diego, CA 92110; (619) 523-5441; torpasta.com; Italian; $$. Located in the Point Loma area, Devine Pastabilities has reinvented the conventional sandwich and turned it into an extraordinary Italian creation. This winner of "Best Sandwich Shop in San Diego" features its signature dish, Torpasta, a delicious Italian roll that is hollowed, perfectly toasted, and stuffed with amazing Italian entrees. It's hard to beat a sandwich made with Italian sausage, onion, bell pepper, and penne in marinara stuffed into a large torpedo roll. Most menu items are also available as traditional Italian meals, served on a plate. Other unique combinations offered daily include fettuccine Alfredo with broccoli, spaghetti and meatballs, vegetarian favorites, and more. Also choose from traditional torpedo sandwiches and pizzas, or one of the unique Torsalads served on a roll. There is also a small selection of wine and draft or bottled beer.

El Jardín Cantina, 2885 Perry Rd, San Diego, CA 92106; (619) 795-2322; eljardincantina.com; Mexican; $$. Located in Liberty Station, this unique eatery lends a laidback atmosphere idyllic for sipping signature margaritas and indulging in piquant Mexican dishes. Guests are welcomed into the massive 8,000-square-foot space under a bright canopy of colorful umbrellas and lush greenery, setting the mood for a picturesque dinner on the expansive outdoor patio space. The colors and feel of the patio continue inside thanks to a living plant wall, pops of bright blue from deep velvet booths, and a multi-tired, multi-colored light fixture. El Jardín Cantina offers dishes such as Lamb Barbacoa, Pollo En Mole, a variety of guacamole options, and a selection of specialty tacos sure to please any palate. For those looking to try a few different flavors, 'flights' are offered for the guacamole options, Mariscos, and even margaritas. There are several vegan options on the menu, including a Portobello Mushroom taco, or the Coco Veracruz, made with lime marinated coconut, Veracruz salsa, green olives, capers, and cilantro. Thanks to an open-air kitchen, guests sitting indoors can watch the culinary team at work. Wine lovers will find several varietal options from Valle de Guadalupe, among other regions, available by the glass or the bottle.

Feast and Fareway, 2000 Visalia Row, Coronado, CA 92118; (619) 996-3322; feastandfarewaycoronado.com; American; $$. This breakfast, lunch and dinner concept at the Coronado Golf Course was designed with the local community in mind, serving golfers, Coronado visitors and locals alike. Enjoy two separate bar areas, as well as massive floor-length windows which allow for stunning views of the golf course and Coronado Bridge. The menu includes unique creations such as Duck Mac & Cheese.

Humphreys by the Bay, 2241 Shelter Island Drive, San Diego, CA 92106; (619) 378-4281; humphreysrestaurant.com; California Modern; $$$. With stunning views of the marina and a casual- but-upscale vibe, Humphreys is a great destination. Unlike most other restaurants in San Diego, this location is also host to major concerts from April through September right on the hotel property. There's no better way to spend a warm summer evening than dining under the stars and enjoying top-tier entertainment. Some of the biggest acts to visit San Diego will use Humphreys as their venue. But what about the food? The menu is packed with items that celebrate many global cuisines and flavors. Their brunch is considered one of the best in San Diego, offering everything from the traditional breakfast, carving station, pastas, and dessert fare to upscale choices including ceviche, sushi rolls, steamed mussels, and oysters. The dinner menu is extensive and offers something for everyone. One of the more popular dishes is the blackened jidori chicken, with piccholine olive potato puree and pancetta-blue cheese sauce.

Ikiru Sushi, 2850 Womble Rd., San Diego, CA 92106; (619) 221-1228; libertystation.com; Japanese; $$. This quaint little Japanese restaurant is located in the heart of Liberty Station and offers a relaxing break from the hustle and bustle of shopping nearby. Lunchtime is especially crowded, with many of the businesspeople stopping by for a quick sushi fix or lunch special before heading back to work. In addition to the items you would expect, such as sushi/sashimi, hand rolls, and specialty rolls, the broad menu includes many other traditional Japanese meat and seafood dishes, such as Teriyaki, Yakisoba, Udon, Katsu, and Ramen. Their full bar features a variety of sake and Japanese beers. They even offer an online ordering and delivery menu for convenience.

Island Prime/C-Level Lounge, 880 Harbor Island Drive, San Diego, CA 92101; (619) 298-6802; islandprime.com; American; $$$$. Resting on stilts atop San Diego Bay overlooking the city skyline and Coronado, this is one of my favorite restaurants. Not just for the view, but mainly because I am a huge fan of Executive Chef and Partner Deborah Scott. I've visited many restaurant kitchens in my career, and they often get messy and chaotic, but not for Scott. She runs a tight ship, and her kitchen is the cleanest I've ever seen. She has a unique flare for making guests feel at home. The C-Level is a more relaxed dining experience, primarily on an open patio, offering both lunch and dinner. Island Prime is the more sophisticated sibling, offering upscale indoor dining focused on high-end meats. No matter which side you choose, the meals are excellent in quality, presentation, and taste. One of my favorites is the Island Prime double pork chop with brown sugar crust, Gruyere au gratin potatoes, apple pearl onion chutney, wild boar bacon, and apple-mustard demi. One of the most popular C-Level items is the crusted ahi tuna, with Chinese black rice, pineapple salsa, wasabi, and soy-ginger reduction.

Jimmy's Famous American Tavern, 4990 N. Harbor Dr., San Diego, CA 92106; (619) 226-2103; j-fat.com; American; $$$. Come here for a bottle of Old Rasputin Imperial Stout and a big burger (so big that you'll hardly finish). Located on the Marina, it's a great place to relax and enjoy the view. More than just a neighborhood tavern, this local hot spot has some innovative food to go with their great drinks. Plenty of excellent beer choices are available on tap and by the bottle, as well as a selection of wines by the glass or bottle. One of the more popular signature drinks is Jimmy's Bramble, with True lemon vodka, fresh squeezed lime and grapefruit juices, simple syrup, and muddled blackberries. Since early childhood, Jimmy has been learning to create simple foods that he describes as "authentic, real, delicious comfort food for the foodie." His burgers are some of the best in town. The Spicy California Burger, a half- pound of Creekstone Farms Black Angus Beef, with Jack cheese, avocado, pickled jalapeños, and herb aioli is amazing. Every burger is served with wonderfully seasoned French fries, peanut slaw, or simple greens. The burger is so big, it comes to your table with a huge steak knife driven though the center. Another popular favorite is the Buttermilk Fried Chicken Breast, served crispy on the outside and juicy on the inside, with mashed potatoes and famous thyme cream gravy. Delicious!

Latin Chef, 1142 Garnet Ave., San Diego, CA 92109; (858) 270-8810; latinchefsandiego.com; Latin American; $$. Take a seat in this small Pacific Beach restaurant and get ready for something different, as Peruvian cuisine is not easy to find in San Diego. Located on busy Garnet Avenue in Pacific Beach, parking can be somewhat of a challenge, but worth the extra effort. The unique blend of flavors incorporates European, African, Asian, and Incan influences. More recently, they have added several Brazilian dishes at the behest of their loyal patrons, who often pack into the dining room on any given day. All of the dishes I've sampled are unique and interesting for my Mediterranean-born palate. One of their specialties is the seco de carne de res, a thick beef stew bursting with flavors and served with beans and rice. Another excellent dish is the aji de gallina, pulled chicken meat cooked with a creamy aji amarillo sauce and served over boiled potatoes. Be sure to save room for one of their exceptional desserts. Their marketplace includes a variety of Peruvian foods and ingredients available to take home.

Leroy's Kitchen and Lounge, 1015 Orange Avenue, Coronado, CA 92118; (619) 437-6087; leroyskitchenandlounge.com; American; $$$. This newer establishment in Coronado is reasonably priced for the normally expensive Coronado location. Grab a seat in the open-air dining room or at the busy bar and lounge. Specializing in seasonal, farm-fresh food from local and sustainable sources, the food at Leroy's is prepared in a way that highlights the ingredients without masking flavors. Discover and enjoy the many pleasures of a globally influenced menu with unique flavor pairings, such as grilled local yellowtail with arugula pesto, porter-braised short ribs with creamy polenta or Duroc bone-in pork chop with maple bourbon glaze and ginger pears. Experience irresistible local craft beers, and craft cocktails made with unique ingredients, including ginger beer, chipotle vodka, and rose water.

Moo Time Creamery, 1025 Orange Ave., Coronado, CA 92118; (619) 435-2422; mootime.com; Desserts; $. Some things remain the same throughout the years—one of those things is my love of ice cream. I can't think of a better place to enjoy that creamy frozen treat than on on historic Orange Avenue just steps from the Pacific Ocean. Over 40 flavors of handcrafted ice cream, sorbet, and low-fat frozen yogurt are available. They also have great seasonal flavors during the holidays, like pumpkin, peppermint stick, and my favorite eggnog. Once you've chosen the base, you can also personalize your taste, with plenty of mixes available to create a unique flavor or crunch. The waffle cones are cooked and rolled while you watch, and melt in your mouth. They also have plenty of cake and pie choices, like Kahlua brownie or strawberry cheesecake. It's a sinful indulgence that must be satisfied!

Old Venice, 2910 Canon St., Point Loma, CA 92106; (619) 222-5888; oldvenicerestaurant.com; Italian; $$$. Family owned and operated for over 30 years, this venerable restaurant gives you a taste of Old Italy but is located in the heart of Point Loma and just minutes from Shelter Island, the airport, and major freeways. The warm Venetian decor features stark white walls, hanging chandeliers, flickering candlelight, and a covered brick patio in the back of the restaurant. The patio is especially romantic in the evenings, when small lights flicker along the walls, on your table, and around a large tree. Love is always in the air, where you'll see couples feeding each other pasta while sipping on Chianti, or large families reveling in conversation. The Bolognese sauce features an earthy and garlicky richness that's perfect over rigatoni. I have a soft spot for cheese-filled ravioli, which taste like the ones from my mother's kitchen. Other local favorites include the veal saltimbocca and chicken cacciatori. Live music is offered on weekend nights, making it the most popular time to visit, so be sure to call ahead for reservations.

Peohe's, 1201 1st St., Coronado, CA 92118; (619) 437-4474; peohes.com; Seafood; $$$$. Located on the water's edge in the Coronado Ferry Landing Marketplace, this is one of the most romantic restaurants on Coronado. In a casual, elegant dining room with views of the downtown skyline and San Diego bay through floor-to-ceiling windows, diners savor fresh tropical seafood dishes influenced by Pacific Rim flavors. The natural essence of the sea is evident in unexpected menu offerings such as crab-stuffed tilapia with a caper butter sauce, pan-seared jumbo scallops finished in a ginger-orange sesame glaze, and crispy wok-fried whole bass served with a hot and spicy Thai sauce. A sushi bar entices patrons with inventive rolls and contemporary sushi creations. Peohe's is easily accessible by land or water—just a 5-minute trip from downtown via private yacht or water taxi, and a 10-minute automobile ride over the Coronado Bay Bridge.

Pomodoro Ristorante Italiano, 2833 Avenida De Portugal, San Diego, CA 92106; (619) 523-1301; pomodorosd.com; Italian; $$$. Taking inspiration from a primary ingredient, Pomodoro Ristorante boasts a decor that features more than one nod to that master fruit, the tomato. With curtains hanging over the dining room's large windows and accent pieces that could have come from Grandmother's home, Pomodoro is both casual and comfortable. Fresh house-made pastas and sauces drive in that home-away-from-home feeling, while the full menu of sumptuous steak, seafood, and chicken specialties confirms you're in a special place indeed. One of the better menu items is the Gamberi Pomodoro, a wonderful mix of shrimp sautéed with artichokes and mushrooms in a light tomato sauce. The heated patio makes dining alfresco a possibility any time, especially with the Point Loma breezes beckoning us out to play.

Serea, 1500 Orange Ave., Coronado, CA 92118; (619) 522-8490; hoteldel.com; California Modern; $$$$. Everyone agrees that the Hotel del Coronado is a legendary landmark in San Diego. That places a lot of pressure on its signature restaurant, 1500 Ocean, to deliver unparalleled excellence. No visit to this city would be complete without dining at this upscale eatery, mere steps from the Pacific Ocean, and offering both indoor and terraced seating. There's something special about dining in a location that has become a flagship picture for the city, not to mention the view is hard to duplicate. This culinary paradise offers only the freshest cuisine, primarily sourced from local farmers and producers. The wine and craft beer list is extensive, offering an endless list of options from every major region of the world, ranging from reasonable to extravagant. The menu is filled with items that will appeal to all of your senses. Their daily selection of oysters is one of the best in the city. For dinner, choose one of the daily fresh fish offerings, or the tasting menu to sample a variety of items.

Slater's 50/50 Burgers by Design, 2750 Dewey Road, San Diego, CA 92106; (619) 398-2600; slaters5050.com; Burgers; $$. If you are a burger lover, head straight into the heart of the happiest burger place on earth! No frills here, just a wide-open and modern burger joint that offers novelty burgers that are hard to beat. Best of all, guests can design their own burger in a variety of creative ways. Choose from patties made with beef, turkey, or their signature 50/50 (50 percent ground beef and 50 percent ground bacon) patty. The veggie patty is also extremely good. Slater's also showcases an abundance of accouterments, including 12 cheeses, 30 toppings, and 20 sauces. Don't miss the Flaming Hot Burger; a fiery beef patty compressed in between a ciabatta roll with fire- roasted green chilies, pepper jack cheese, and chipotle mayo, seductively topped off with beer-battered onion rings. With 111 brewskies on tap, you'll have no trouble cooling off your tongue. On any given day, there are about 40 craft brews from San Diego, with the remainder coming from all over the world. Additional location is at 2750 Dewey Rd #193, San Diego, CA 92106.

Solare Ristorante; Liberty Station, 2820 Roosevelt Rd., #104., San Diego, CA 92106; (619) 270-9670; solarelounge.com; Italian; $$$. Located in Point Loma's Liberty Station, this unique Italian eatery offers diners the option to dine in an intimate dining room, private wine room, open-air patio, or lounge. The authentic Italian menu features fresh and locally sourced ingredients, including wild fish and hormone free meat. Don't miss the Lasagna House-Made Lasagna with slow braised Bolognese sauce or the Hand-Crafted Ravioli filled with spinach and ricotta. Touted as a Solare epic experience, you might want to opt for the Whole Suckling Pig Feast, which is served family style. It consists of a whole 14 to 16-pound pig prepared Sardinian style, and serves approximately 10-12 people.

Tender Greens, 2400 Historic Decatur Rd., San Diego, CA 92106; (619) 226-6254; tendergreensfood.com; Organic/Health Food; $$. This is a cafeteria-style first come, first serve organic restaurant where you order your food at one end and pay at the other end and seat yourself. The menu offers big salads, comforting soups, fresh sandwiches, and grilled meats. Breads are made fresh daily by artisan bakeries and the finest quality ingredients are used in the food, including cold-pressed olive oils, ground spices, mustards, vinegars, and cheeses, as well as desserts made on-site. Enjoy rotating house-cured meats, especially handcrafted salamis and prosciutto. The beef comes from grain-fed hormone/antibiotic-free cows and free-range chickens. Even the tuna is line caught from the Pacific. Savor wines from local boutique wineries, as well as great microbrews and organic teas. Multiple locations can be found throughout San Diego.

Downtown, Little Italy

This compact district along India Avenue in downtown was once home to nearly 6,000 Italian families that worked to establish San Diego as the center of the tuna industry. Since the decline of this industry in the mid-1900s, Little Italy has now become the largest and oldest continuous ethnic neighborhood in San Diego. Centrally located between the waterfront and I-5, this urban district is easy to access, with plenty of street parking available. The streets are lined with vintage and modern buildings that house ground-floor restaurants, shops, and boutiques, anchoring multiple levels of condos, townhomes, and businesses.

Although the area has a variety of cuisines available, it primarily serves the visitor looking for everything Italian. From bakeries to delis, take-out pizza to high-end dining rooms, you'll find a taste to please every craving. Park yourself in one of the bistro tables, order an espresso with a pastry, and watch the bustling street-life pass by.

The Neighborhood Association is well known for its engagement, hosting regular events to support this vibrant community. The Mercado is a weekly farmers' market that draws huge crowds, including many of the local chefs who pride themselves with including local produce and freshly caught fish on their menus. Although a number of festivals are hosted throughout the year, none is more popular than the Little Italy Festa in October, one of the largest Italian festivals outside of New York City. You can enjoy endless food options, entertainment, arts and crafts, street painting, stickball, and bocce ball tournaments.

Assenti's Pasta, 2044 India St., San Diego, CA 92101; (619) 239-5117; assentispasta.com; Grocery/Market; $$. Handmade pasta is the big seller at this Italian shop in Little Italy. Umberto and Adriana Assenti's pastas are made of a combination of semolina, durum, and wheat flours, water, and eggs (pasta al'ouvo), which makes the flavor and texture very delicate. There are no artificial flavors, colors, or preservatives in any of their homemade food products. All pasta is sold by the pound, which serves approximately three people. All of the sauces are homemade, and I love their pesto sauce over fettuccine. Choose from a fresh selection of deli meats, sliced to your satisfaction. Assenti's also carries a wide variety of imported Italian olive oils, anchovies, biscotti, imported olives, and other specialty items. Be sure to also taste their homemade desserts—tiramisu and cannoli, especially around the holiday season (when eating sweets is deemed acceptable) are divine.

Bayside Kitchen + Bar, 2137 Pacific Highway, San Diego, CA 92101; (619) 819-0090; baysidekitchenandbar.com; New American; $$$. This 4,100 square-foot restaurant, offering picturesque views of the harbor and bayside, celebrates a menu rich with fresh produce from local farmers and nearby purveyors. A distinctive collection of house made cocktails is served in unique glassware, such as mini milk and mason jars. It's fun to dine at one of the two 16-foot long communal tables or in the adjoining courtyard featuring a 20-foot linear fire pit. For starters don't miss the Penn Cove Mussels, Chicken Liver Mousse, and Harvest Farro Salad. Popular favorites for dinner include the Lamb Ragu, Steak Frites, and Fish & Chips.

Bencotto Italian Kitchen, 750 W. Fir St., San Diego, CA 92101; (619) 450-4786; lovebencotto.com; Italian; $$. Located in the new "Q" building in the heart of Little Italy, a young generation of Italians, motivated from their experiences from the restaurant business in Milan, Modena, New York, and San Diego, succeeded in creating a modish, relaxed, and appealing kitchen-restaurant. "Bencotto" means and refers to a meal "done well," or perfectly cooked, and that is exactly what you'll get. Menu items are designed to share, so that guests can casually pick and choose from a nice variety of home-style dishes. I've eaten Italian food all my life, and given that pastas are their signature dish, I am happy to report that the pasta here is the real deal. Get Pasta A Modo Tuo (pasta your way) by opting for either pasta fatta a mano (daily hand-made) for a smooth consistency, or pasta artigianale (artisanal) for an "al dente" texture. With a variety of pasta sauces to choose from, my favorite is the pesto with basil, Parmesan, pecorino, pine nuts, and garlic. Craving a little risotto with a lot of cheese? Make a reservation in advance for your special occasion or private party to get a taste of their creamy risotto recipe served tableside from a carved-out wheel of Parmigiano Reggiano.

Bobboi Natural Gelato, 2175 Kettner Blvd, San Diego, CA 92101; (858) 255-8693; bobboi.com/kettner-blvd; Gelato; $. Bobboi Natural Gelato is located on the corner of Kettner Boulevard and Ivy Street in Little Italy. The shop, within the AV8 apartment building, joins Bobboi's stand at the Little Italy Food Hall in providing authentic, high-quality, artisanal gelato to the community that follows a strict seasonal calendar to ensure each flavor stays true to its ingredients. Along with its original La Jolla shop that opened in 2014, this location marks the fast-growing brand's third San Diego area location. Bobboi's new Kettner shop serves 18 of its from-scratch, Italian-meets-Californian-style gelato and sorbet flavors made from seasonal and organic ingredients seven days a week. While Bobboi's stand in the Little Italy Food Hall is a compact iteration of the beloved gelateria, the Kettner Boulevard location boasts 1,000 square feet of gelato goodness. The expanded menu includes signature flavors like Pistachio, Chocolate Caramel and Dark Chocolate Sorbet, along with its more unexpected flavors, from Pumpkin Amaretto (made with organic pumpkin, organic pumpkin spices and amaretto cookies) to Rose Almond (local Hopkins almonds and Lebanese rosewater). There is also an espresso bar serving drinks and affogatos. Bobboi's signature Pozzetti gelato case hides the gelato away to maintain the exact temperature needed to serve up only the freshest gelato. The unique space features colorful accents like bright tile plus indoor-outdoor seating.

Born & Raised, 1909 India St, San Diego, CA 92101; (619) 202-4577; bornandraisedsteak.com; Steakhouse; $$$$. One of the best restaurants in San Diego, Born & Raised pays homage to America's greatest dining institution, the classic steakhouse. The two-story, 10,000 square-foot restaurant has a unique midcentury architectural influence. The custom layout features two oversized bars, and three dedicated dining spaces including the main dining room, a downstairs patio seating, and a 1,500 square-foot rooftop terrace with an adjacent 2,000 square-foot open-air urban garden that grows many of the restaurant's herbs and produce. Born & Raised also operates its own dry-aging program on-site.

Buon Appetito, 1609 India St., San Diego, CA 92101; (619) 238-9880; buonappetitosandiego.com; Italian; $$$. It's an Italian celebration of food, wine, and art at this alluring eatery in Little Italy. Original art pieces are featured on the walls from a special artist every other month. They've sweetened up the escarole, a somewhat bitter lettuce, ever so slightly with an insalata (salad) combination of sliced pears, Gorgonzola, and raspberry vinaigrette. I am a big fan of any kind of meat sauce, typically known as ragu, so I always choose the fusilli pasta topped with a slow-simmered homemade ragu of duck. They also make a fantastic cioppino with fresh clams, mussels, calamari, scallops, fresh fish, and shrimp in a zesty tomato broth. A wine bar attached to the restaurant features a nice selection of vino from around the world.

Cafe Gratitude, 1980 Kettner Blvd., San Diego, CA 92101; (619) 736-5077; cafegratitude.com; Vegan; $$. Rock A Vegan Attitude At Cafe Gratitude! Think 100% organic plant-based gourmet vegan cuisine. Seasonal ingredients for the menu are sourced from local farmers at the peak of freshness. With dishes named after affirmations such as "I Am Free" or "I Am Marvelous", you can't help but feel happy and healthy, even before you take that first bite. I feel "Gracious" when I feast on the Autumn Grain Salad made with butternut squash, radicchio, cashew mozzarella, garbanzo beans, sun-dried tomato pistachio pesto and quinoa. The Eggplant Parmesan Panini is truly "Awesome" with marinara, cashew ricotta, brazil nut parmesan, wild arugula, slow-fermented ciabatta, and mixed greens with fig balsamic vinaigrette. And I admit to "surrendering" to the Gluten-Free Brownie with vanilla coconut cashew ice cream, cashew cream, chocolate sauce, and powdered sugar. Cafe Gratitude's daily operations are conducted according to the principle of "Sacred Commerce," offering diners healthy food in a healthy environment, and encouraging them to adopt a perspective of gratitude. Originally founded in 2004 in San Francisco, Café Gratitude has three locations in Los Angeles (Downtown Arts District, Larchmont Village and Venice Beach), as well as restaurants in Santa Cruz, Berkeley, and Newport Beach.

Cafe Zucchero, 1731 India St., San Diego, CA 92101; (619) 531-1731; cafezucchero.com; Italian; $$$. If you're looking for authentic Italian pastries, this is the place to visit, especially in the morning when all of the delicious treats are fresh out of the kitchen. Everything is handmade in this cute little coffee shop that includes adequate seating inside and plenty of espresso steaming behind the counter. A long glass case lining an entire wall is the centerpiece, showcasing some of the best Italian confections in San Diego. It's nearly impossible to pick just one item, but if I had to choose, it would be the creamy-smooth Strawberry Napoleon. Breakfast and lunch are the busy hours, but they are also open for a casual dinner, offering salads, pizzas, and pastas. Live music is common, and on any given night you'll find a number of the regular patrons stopping by to sing their favorite Italian melody. Unlike the typical karaoke bar, no one reads lyrics on a screen while squawking off-tone. The gentlemen here sing every song by heart, and in a manner that will have you dreaming of gondola rides in Venice.

Cloak & Petal, 1953 India Street, San Diego, CA 92101; (619) 501-5505; cloakandpetal.com; Japanese; $$$$. Showcasing a "hanami-inspired" cherry tree, Cloak & Petal offers Japanese artful dishes that feature fresh sushi, sashimi and nigari. With an atmosphere reminiscent of an abandoned Tokyo subway, diners are transported to an underworld suggestive of a place once forgotten. Popular Japanese small plates include Yuzu Kosho Jidori Wings and Spicy Salmon Battera, as well as shareable combination platters.

The Crack Shack, 2266 Kettner Blvd., San Diego, CA 92101; (619) 795-3299; crack-shack.com; American; $$. Celebrity Chef Richard Blais offers fried chicken and eggs made with ingredients that a Michelin star restaurant would use at The Crack Shack in the Little Italy neighborhood of San Diego. Think Jidori chicken, fresh eggs, and local produce from southern California farms and purveyors. The Crack Shack was literally a miniature metal shack, before Blais turned it into a restaurant with a notable outdoor ambiance. Hang out with your friends, play Bocce or enjoy a cocktail by the fire pit. Blais keeps an eye on his menu, and stays focused on finding the absolute best, local ingredients he can buy. Don't miss the Senor Croque; one of their most popular sandwiches that captures the intersection of chicken and eggs with must have miso maple butter. Another popular favorite is the Chicken Oysters that consist of dark, tender pieces of chicken with an oyster-like taste and size. Additional location is at 407 Encinitas Blvd, Encinitas, CA 92024.

Craft and Commerce, 675 W. Beech St., San Diego, CA 92101; (619) 269-2202; craft-commerce.com; American; $$$. The outside of this restaurant is covered in ivy and inside there's a country- meets-modern house feel with very dim lighting and candlelight. The ceiling is made from restored wood, with restored wood tables and bright orange steel chairs. Inside the walls there are piles and piles of hardbound classic novels, definitely giving you something to think about. I couldn't find any cookbooks here, but was very pleased with their contemporary take on seasonal American cuisine focused on quality-driven fare and a flavor-unique concept. Savor house-made sauces of garlic aioli, spicy aioli, and whole-grain mustard, to name a few. You haven't lived until you've tried the dry-rubbed smoked ribs with jalapeño spoon bread or the fried chicken with buttermilk slaw. If you feel like vegetarian, order the Farmers Plate, a selection of market vegetables and grains that changes weekly. Choose from various craft beers from all over the world with almost 30 rotating taps. A weekend brunch showcases cocktails available in punch bowls and plates designed for sharing.

Curadero, 1047 Fifth Ave #100, San Diego, CA 92101; (619) 515-3003; curadero.com; Mexican; $$$. Curadero (derived from Curandero, or native healer) offers the bold flavors of soulful Mexican cuisine. Enjoy local, sustainable seafood, including fresh fish and raw items from the Crudo Bar. Opt for dishes from the "Little Cravings" section of the menu, or satisfy your hunger with larger hot plates designed for two or more people to share. The Arriba Room located on the second floor offers a lounge and game room where guests can order from the street-style taco window. Look for menu items such as Sopa de Hongos with mushroom broth, epazote, chile arbol, and oaxaca cheese tostada or Pescado Entero; adobo marinated and charcoal grilled whole fish. Choose from a nice selection of tequilas and mezcals, as well as Mexican craft beers, wines from Baja, and craft cocktails.

Davanti Enoteca, 1655 India St., San Diego, CA 92101; (619)-237-9606; davantienoteca.com; Italian; $$$. Yes, there is such a thing as casual fine dining, and it's happening at this Italian restaurant and wine bar in Little Italy that's slowly but surely building a following and changing my long-held belief that good Italian food can exist in America's Finest City. A dimly lit ambiance, a full bar, semi-loud rock n' roll playing in the background, wood tables adorned with wine glasses begging you to take a sip of vino—all looks good to me! The wide-ranging menu embraces salumi and formaggi (cheese), pizza, pasta, and seafood and meat entrees. Among the dishes, the Ligurian-style baked focaccia with fresh soft cow cheese and honeycomb is the number one seller. Bold flavors are crammed into the Davanti burger with its special blend of beef made in house and you'll get a nice jolt of spice from the giant rigatoni and sausage. The kitchen delivers further with grilled swordfish alla siciliana and the oven-roasted wagyu tri tip. Finish off with an exceptional goat cheese cheesecake with salted caramel. Additional location is at 12955 El Camino Real G3, San Diego, CA 92130.

Filippi's Pizza Grotto, 1747 India St., San Diego, CA 92101; (619) 232-5094; realcheesepizza.com; Pizza; $$. This Little Italy restaurant is expansive, with checkered red-and-white tablecloths and wine bottles hanging in woven baskets on the ceiling. Everyone comes here for the straightforward Italian food in big portions at reasonable prices. The pasta dishes are hearty and hefty, filled with meats, sauces, and cheese. So, if you're counting calories, this may not be the best place for you. The pizzas here are fabulous, with a crispy crust and plenty of toppings. Other popular favorites include lasagna with meat sauce, fettuccine Alfredo, veal scalloppini with mushrooms and wine sauce, or chicken parmigiana. Entrees are served a la carte or as a dinner, including soup, salad, and garlic bread. Great desserts include spumoni, cheesecake, and cannoli. A small retail grocery store is located just inside the front door, and offers a deli with Italian meats, a variety of imported olive oils, pasta, Italian cookies, and much more. Multiple locations can be found throughout San Diego.

Glass Door, 1835 Columbia St., San Diego, CA 92101; (619) 564-3755; portovistasd.com; California Modern; $$$. Situated on the fourth floor of the Porto Vista Hotel, this restaurant offers magnificent views of the downtown waterfront and San Diego Bay. Elevated chairs are situated around communal tables and along the open west wall, which is essentially a lengthy "perch" offering 180-degree views. Colorful glass lanterns of various sorts hang from the ceiling, and enhance the mood when lit in the evenings. This destination is extremely popular in the late afternoons, as patrons collect together to enjoy spectacular sunsets and blinking lights from the nighttime skyline. The menu has California flair but is influenced heavily from several international culinary styles. A great example is the simple but stunning Luca Brasi, a whole fried tilapia served with corn puree, baby carrots, and jalapeño chimichurri. For a Middle Eastern touch, try the tandoori skewer, with spice marinated chicken, pickled vegetables, and fried dough. There is also a long list of small plates, salads, and burgers to satisfy any appetite/palate. Don't forget to sample one of the many signature drinks, featuring house-infused liquors and creative recipes. Also open for brunch on the weekends.

Herb & Wood, 2210 Kettner Blvd, San Diego, CA 92101; (619) 955-8495; herbandwood.com; New American; $$$. Located in San Diego's North Little Italy, Herb & Wood offers a seasonally ingredient driven menu of simple rustic fare cooked from a custom wood-fired oven. Love Pizza? Their homemade dough is aged for 48 hours for a pizza that's charred to perfection. Don't miss their signature Stuffed Branzino with Meyer lemon, parsley, chives, and chervil, wrapped in prosciutto and roasted, with chili tapenade made with Castelvatrano olives, Calabrian chili's, shallots and garlic. Other popular menu items include house made pastas and desserts that complement the cuisine, including Blueberry Soufflé with whipped buttermilk and blueberry compote. The cocktail menu is fun here. Think old-school drinks paired with fresh herbs and other aromatic ingredients.

Indigo Grill, 1536 India St., San Diego, CA 92101; (619) 234-6802; indigogrill.com; California Modern; $$$. Although this compact neighborhood is lined with excellent choices to satisfy your Italian fix, there are a few exceptions. Indigo Grill is a perfect example, drawing its influences from Alaska to Mexico and settling on an identity of Southwestern Fusion cuisine. Stepping past the front door, you'll be greeted by American Indian totems and ancient Mexican runes, offset by modern touches of glass and mosaics. The restaurant is almost always overflowing with patrons' eager to taste the unique blends of flavors in the drinks and food. A good example is the cucumber black pepper martini, a spicy mix of gin, muddled kiwi and lime, and melon liqueur. For dinner, try the Vera Cruz maize tamale or pecan-crusted rainbow trout, both excellent choices to savor the special blend of flavors that only a bright-minded chef like Deborah Scott can create.

Ironside Fish & Oyster, 1654 India St., San Diego, CA 92101; (619) 269-3033; ironsidefishandoyster.com; Seafood; $$$. Named after the previous tenant of the 1920's–era warehouse, Ironside Metal Supply, Ironside Fish and Oyster is the most recent restaurant innovation of executive chef and partner Jason McLeod. Little Italy, which is historically a fishing village, didn't have a single oyster bar or seafood joint amongst its dozens of restaurants. McLeod noted the missing link and decided to make a change. He created a menu chock–full of local seafood, including lobster rolls, clam chowder and a healthy selection of raw bar items such as oysters, clams, uni, abalone and crab claws. The menu also offers a varied choice of soups, salads and sandwiches. Guests can opt for anything from shrimp and pork bahn mi and lobster sliders to fish and chips and beer braised mussels. A daily catch of Mahi Mahi, snapper, yellowtail bass and swordfish is offered grilled or cooked a la plancha.

©Maria Desiderata Montana

Isola Pizza Bar, 1526 India St., San Diego, CA 92101; (619) 255-4230; isolapizzabar.com; Italian; $$$. Savor artisan pizzas made from double-zero flour imported from Napoli, finished in a special pizza oven purchased from the same region. The high heat and less than 5-minute baking time give the pizza crust an authentic spotted appearance. An open kitchen allows diners to observe the chefs at work, and a small outdoor patio is also accessible for those that prefer dining al fresco. A long wall adds to the ambiance, highlighted by shelves filled with wine, imported olive oil, canned supplies, and oak logs for the oven. Popular favorites include the Baked Pasta al Forno with quattro formaggi, saffron, and spicy breadcrumbs and the Sardenaira Ligure, a thicker style pizza with tomato sauce, anchovies, olives, garlic, and oregano. A second location is at 7734 Girard Avenue in La Jolla, CA.

Juniper & Ivy, 2228 Kettner Blvd, San Diego, CA 92101; juniperandivy.com; New American; $$$. Bring your family to Juniper & Ivy, a modernist American restaurant set in a converted 1920s saw tooth warehouse located on the outskirts of San Diego's Little Italy. The Juniper and Ivy kitchen is helmed by Celebrity Chef Richard Blais, winner of Bravo's Top Chef All-Stars and successful restaurateur, cookbook author and television personality. The menu highlight s the region's bountiful and fresh local produce offering unexpected iterations on the classic dishes, including snacks, raw, toast and pasta in addition to plates, both small and large, as well as dessert. My favorites include the Carne Cruda Asada with Quail Egg, Cotija and Jalapeno, White Bass Ceviche with Grapefruit Aguachile, Guajillo, Radish Salsa and Fingerlime or the Wild Boar Bolognese with Black Pepper Rigatoni, Olive Gremolata and Burrata.

Landini's Pizza, 1827 India St., San Diego, CA 92101; (619) 238-3502; landinispizzeria.com; Pizza; $$. Nestled in the heart of San Diego's historic Little Italy you'll find Landini's Pizzeria. Serving New York–style, hand-tossed pizza, this is a great spot to pick up a few slices and enjoy during your walk through the neighborhood. They also serve Paninis layered with imported meats and cheeses, Florentine-inspired pastas, baked dishes, and a fine selection of beers and wines. A very popular item is the Stromboli: pizza dough rolled like a sandwich and stuffed with ham, green pepper, pepperoni, mozzarella, and marinara.

Mimmo's Italian Village, 1743 India St., San Diego, CA 92101; (619) 239-3710; mimmos.biz; Italian; $$. Established for over 40 years in Little Italy, this destination is more than just a restaurant. Step inside and be transported to a small village in Sicily, with a cobblestone walkway and storefronts, complete with faux balconies, lampposts, and planter boxes. The experience is reminiscent of a simpler version of a Las Vegas indoor walkway, sending you to a faraway city without the plane fare. There's also a very generous patio in the front, if you prefer to watch the action along India Street. Lunches are ordered deli style and include a vast array of sandwiches, salads, pastas, and pizzas. The baked eggplant sandwich is a guilty pleasure and the Italian sausage and peppers are delicious. For dinner, it's a great alternative to the higher-priced and fancier establishments in the area. Buy a bottle of wine, a couple of hearty Italian dishes, and enjoy some good conversation. Live music is often scheduled at night, especially on the weekends.

Mona Lisa, 2061 India St., San Diego, CA 92101; (619) 234-4893; monalisalittleitaly.com; Grocery/Market; $$. I like to frequent this popular store and restaurant in Little Italy. The deli has a nice selection of authentic Italian meats including prosciutto bresaola, cappicola, coppa, Genoa salami, pancetta, pepperoni, and sopresatta. My favorite cheeses are always available, especially Parmigiana Reggiano, buffalo mozzarella, and cambozola. I can always find what I am looking for when it comes to Italian cookies, olive oil, Italian wines, and fresh pasta. A limited selection of produce includes tomatoes, apples, lemons, pears, bananas, rapini, lettuce, celery, carrots, mushrooms, eggplant, garlic, onions, avocado, and potatoes. An adjoining restaurant offers a full bar, extensive wine list, and great service in a relaxed and comfortable atmosphere. The restaurant's menu includes pizza, antipasti, hot and cold sandwiches, pasta and ravioli, and house specialties including veal and chicken dishes, lasagna, manicotti, seafood, and more.

Nonna, 1735 India Street, 1735 India St, San Diego, CA 92101; 619-234-1735; nonnasd.com; Italian; $$$. Nonna offers Italian comfort food in the epicenter of Little Italy's India Street. The menu boasts traditional Sicilian cuisine comprised of produce and seafood sourced from local farms and purveyors. Signature dishes include Lasagna with meat ragu and béchamel, and Bucatini Amatriciana with pancetta, onions, pomodoro and pecorino. Choose from a nice selection of pizzas including Margherita and Prosciutto from the restaurant's stone oven.

Petrini's, 610 W. Ash St., San Diego, CA 92101; (619) 595-0322; http://petrinis-sandiego.com/; Italian; $$. Chef-Proprietor David Petrini keeps family and friends at his Italian table with generations-old, tried- and-true family recipes. His "La Famiglia Mangia" ("the family eats") philosophy keeps the diners happy at his warm and welcoming restaurant. There are plenty of windows to enjoy the hustle and bustle of San Diego, but the warm light and candles make you feel at home. The open kitchen adds to the ambiance, and Petrini is often seen wandering through the dining room talking to patrons and enjoying the conversation. Petrini's Italian peasant cuisine is offered three times a day. For breakfast, it's a fig loaf with butter for my Italian coffee and me. For lunch, try the smoked salmon served top thin-crust pizza dough that's lightly brushed with pesto sauce and topped with fresh sliced Roma tomatoes, red onions, capers, and freshly grated Parmigiano Reggiano. For dinner, try the baked penne noodles (ziti) smothered in meat sauce and topped with melted provolone and mozzarella.

Queenstown Public House, 1557 Columbia Street, San Diego, CA 92101; (619) 546-0444; queenstownpublichouse.com; New Zealand Restaurant; $$. Queenstown Public House serves all natural, organic American fare with a New Zealand twist in a cozy and comfortable house-like setting, including the parlor room where you can watch sheep grazing on the ceiling. Sourcing the freshest local ingredients for their mainstay dishes are what guests have come to rely on. A must have is the Parlor Pot Pie, Queenstown's play on the traditional potpie, taken to another level. Inside the skillet, you'll find a puff pastry with the filling layered on the top and a whole game hen tucked inside the middle. Don't miss stopping by this one-of-a-kind restaurant that's been a longtime favorite in San Diego's Little Italy. Watch out though, rumor has it that Wanda, their resident ghost, has been spotted around the property in the early morning and late evening. Seems she's always up to something and likes to keep things interesting for everyone involved. Their sister property is Dunedin North Park, located at 3501 30th St, San Diego, CA 92104.

Salt & Straw, 1670 India Street, San Diego, CA 92101; 1670 India Street; (619) 542-9394; saltandstraw.com; Ice Cream; $$. This iconic Portland-based, family-run ice cream purveyor offers fan favorites including Sea Salt with Caramel Ribbons, Almond Brittle with Salted Ganache, and Honey Lavender, as well as a special menu created just for San Diego featuring local artisans such as James Coffee and Belching Beaver Brewery. Scoops are available in either cups or handmade waffle cones, in addition to milkshakes, special sundaes, and pints to go (insider tip: customers can always skip the line when buying a pint!). A second location is now open in One Paseo on Del Mar Heights Road.

Zinqué - San Diego, 2101 Kettner Blvd, San Diego, CA 92101; (619) 915-6172; lezinque.com; French: $$. This French bistro, café and wine bar, known for its iconic locations in Venice, West Hollywood, Newport Beach, and Downtown Los Angeles, is housed at AV8, a mixed-use retail and residential development in San Diego's Little Italy, on the corner of Kettner Boulevard and West Hawthorn Street. Guests can relax in a chic interior designed with a central bar, wooden tables, fireplace, wrought-iron windows and a covered street-side patio. Like the restaurant's sibling locations in Southern California, Zinqué offers an impressive menu of craft cocktails and French staples. The bistro offers the best in French cuisine, including authentic Parisian bread imported from the famous Poilâne Bakery in Paris, and coffee brewed with beans from La Colombe, the world-renowned coffee roasters. Zinqué also serves classic cheeses, and will craft only the finest charcuterie selections. With an emphasis on organic and sustainable wines, the extensive wine list is carefully selected and features French wines as well as unique producers from around the world.

Gaslamp Quarter, East Village & Seaport Village

This area is hands-down the heartbeat of San Diego tourism. With hundreds of restaurants, nightclubs, shops, boutiques, and major hotels within an 8-block radius, you would never need another destination for the San Diego experience. Encompassing the lower-downtown area and stretching to the bay, a good pair of walking shoes will allow you to journey through the action, both day and night. Victorian-era buildings are densely packed along the street and intermingle with modern hotel entrances, compact restaurant patios, nightclubs, and shop fronts. It is truly a place to lose yourself in the action.

Born in the mid-1800s, this area along the waterfront was a centerpiece of what was to become San Diego. However, it wasn't until the mid-1900s that a major renovation took place, transforming what had become a neighborhood of ill repute into a shopping and entertainment mecca. In more recent times, the Gaslamp is an epicurean's paradise, with virtually every international cuisine available in high-end dining rooms, to budget hole-in-the-wall's. Parking can be a challenge, but the Horton Plaza (named after one of the first land owners, Alonzo Horton) offers 3-hour validation in a high-rise parking garage adjacent to the largest shopping mall in downtown. Better yet, stay at one of the fine downtown hotels and bypass the parking headache. Everything you need is within walking distance.

Seaport Village encompasses 14 acres of waterfront shopping and dining, with cobblestone pathways intertwined among lush landscapes and some of the best Bay views in the city. Waterfront eateries are a popular destination year-round.

East Village is one of the largest and fastest-growing neighborhoods in the downtown area, primarily fueled by the opening of Petco Park, a uniquely centered baseball stadium that is home to the San Diego Padres. Once an old warehouse district, it has quickly become a destination for visitors and residents who crave living in a vibrant urban environment.

©*Maria Desiderata Montana*

BESHOCK Ramen, 1288 Market St, San Diego, CA 92101; (619) 501-9612; be-shock.com; Japanese; $$. Stemming from the Japanese word for "the beauty of food" or "gastronomy," BESHOCK is a trendy addition to San Diego's diverse restaurant scene in East Village. This culturally inspired eatery offers authentic Japanese cuisine and a lighter take on ramen. Love sake? The restaurant's sake selection is crafted around the restaurant's menu items. Don't miss the BESHOCK Buns, Spicy Miso Ramen, or the Tiramisu Shaved Ice for dessert.

Cafe Sevilla, 353 5th Ave., San Diego, CA 92101; (619) 233-5979; cafesevilla.com; Latin American; $$$. First opened in 1987, Cafe Sevilla is easily one of the most entertaining establishments in the San Diego area. An exhibition kitchen, tapas bar, and underground club adds to the fun. Once you browse the menu, you'll quickly realize that multiple visits will be necessary to sample the extensive tapas selection. Every dish has its own personality, and the flavors are exceptional. I highly recommend the braised Basque rabbit and black paella en su tinta, with Bomba black rice, mixed seafood, and aioli drizzle. But no visit would be complete without enjoying the weekly Flamenco dinner show, including authentic Flamenco and gypsy musicians and dancers. In addition, the nightclub is open 7 days a week with live music and dancing.

Cowboy Star Restaurant & Butcher Shop, 640 10th Avenue, San Diego, CA 92101; (619) 450-5880; thecowboystar.com; Steak House; $$$. Experience an inimitable cuisine that embodies the spirit of the American West while utilizing the season's freshest offerings in a warm and welcoming atmosphere complete with exposed beam ceilings, cowboy accents, and classic landscape photography. A display kitchen allows guests to get an up-close and personal view of the chefs in action, and an adjoining walk-in retail butcher shop is the source for the signature meat served in the restaurant. All meats are brought in from farms and ranches that adhere to the highest integrity farming practices, include 100 percent grass and corn-fed, USDA Prime, 35-day dry-aged beef along with several free-range poultry and game options. Cowboy Star sources only the freshest ingredients for each and every dish, utilizing farmers' markets to find the best produce available. Their seafood program also follows the strict Monterey Bay Aquarium's "Seafood Watch" to ensure total sustainability in an effort to save the oceans. I am crazy about their signature hand-chopped steak tartare prepared to order with capers, shallots, and parsley then topped with a quail egg and served with toasted baguette.

Dough Nations, 1985 National Ave #1101, San Diego, CA 92113; (619) 487-0802; doughnationsd.com; Pizza; $. Nestled in San Diego's Barrio Logan neighborhood, Dough Nations is a 2,500-square-foot restaurant with indoor and patio seating for 77 guests. The menu includes classic Italian and internationally-inspired appetizers, salads, sandwiches, pizzas and pastas. Pizzas are available by the slice or whole pie. Dough Nations also features a full bar complete with cocktails, wine and beer.

Grant Grill, 326 Broadway, U.S. Grant Hotel, San Diego, CA 92101; (619) 744-2077; grantgrill.com; California Modern; $$$$. This is fine dining at its best, with attentive service and classic touches of wood paneling, cream linens, and soft candlelight. The Grant Grill served its first mock turtle soup in 1951. Still serving it today, every bite of this rich and beefy tomato-based soup, with a touch of sherry poured tableside, is a sumptuous journey through time. Breakfast, lunch, and dinner are available daily. The large bar area is a perfect location for after-work relaxing or setting the mood for a great evening. Live music is playing regularly, and the happy hours can get very crowded. Executive Chef Mark Kropczynski highlights their ever-evolving menu with local produce, fresh seafood, and prime meats. For dinner, I would strongly recommend you splurge on the tasting menu, a rotating combination of 3 to 5 chef specialties paired with fantastic wines.

Greystone the Steakhouse, 658 5th Ave., San Diego, CA 92101; (619) 232-0225; greystonesteakhouse.com; Steak House; $$$$. Located in the historically landmarked Rivoli Theater building from the 1920s, this award-winning steak house was renamed The Bijou Theatre and operated by Pussycat Theatres, which screened adult films in the early 1970s. Today, this spacious, multilevel restaurant features a suave and sophisticated ambiance perfect for any occasion. A nightly dinner menu features aged steaks, fresh seafood, and homemade pastas, along with an extensive wine list. More than a steak house, exotic game selections include roasted elk chop and buffalo tenderloin. Other great choices include a slow simmered Kobe beef short rib, bourbon brined pork chop, and lamb chops. Pair your meat with a nice selection of sauces including béarnaise, bordelaise, truffle zabayon, Armagnac and green peppercorn, and whole-grain mustard Chardonnay.

Lola 55, 1290 F St, San Diego, CA 92101; (619) 542-9155; lola55.com; Mexican; $$. Not your ordinary taco joint, this 3,200-square-foot restaurant serves Mexican gastronomic fare steeped in regional tradition. Highlights include Ribeye Carne Asada, Pork Belly Al Pastor and Spicy Smoked Fish. The corn tortillas are made from scratch and pressed to order right before guests. There are plenty of other options on the menu including aguachile, ceviche tostaditas, mesquite grilled elote and pozole verde. A well-curated list of libations mirrors the restaurant's culinary philosophy, and includes citrus-focused elements to balance the menu's spice-forward dishes.

Lotus Thai, 906 Market St., San Diego, CA 92101; (619) 595-0115; lotusthaisd.com; Thai; $$$. If you're looking for a more tranquil destination among the hustle and bustle of downtown, this is definitely the place. Lotus serves upscale Thai cuisine in a dining room meant to create a soothing and relaxed environment. Take your seat next to a Buddha statue and enjoy the warm wood accents and tropical plants. The extensive menu offers something for everyone, whether you're a vegetarian or meat-lover. I am a sucker for their fresh and tasty spring rolls to start my meal, but another great choice is the Lotus Platter appetizer, which includes a sampling of their 5 most popular starters. Other favorites include the spicy eggplant, with Thai basil, onions, carrots, and a white bean sauce; or the flaming-hot Crying Tiger, with charcoal-broiled marinated prime steak, a spicy lime dipping sauce, and mixed greens. To cool your palate, consider the luscious fried banana and ice cream for dessert. Additional location is at 3761 Sixth Ave, San Diego, CA 92103.

Lucky's Lunch Counter, 338 7th Ave., San Diego, CA 92101; (619) 255-4782; luckyslunchcounter.com; American; $$. Situated in the expansive and famed Culy Warehouse in Downtown San Diego, Lucky's Lunch Counter offers nostalgic eats in an easygoing atmosphere, just steps away from Petco Park in the East Village. Built to evoke memories of the old-style ballpark counters from the early 1900s, their most popular fare is overstuffed sandwiches and vintage hot dogs. Fast casual cuisine is the name of the game here. Breakfast is served all day, including a build-your-own omelet or burrito. Their hot pastrami or crispy pork tenderloin over-stuffed sandwiches are spectacular! No visit would be complete without tasting their original firedog or bratwurst, split, grilled, and just waiting for you to dress up any way you like. Plenty of salad choices are also available. Be sure to stop in before or after one of the San Diego Padres home games, when Lucky's will reward you with a game-day special.

Nobu, 207 5th Ave., San Diego, CA 92101; (619) 814-4124; noburestaurants.com; Asian Fusion; $$$$. Located inside the Hard Rock Hotel San Diego, Nobu launched in November 2007. Executive Chef-Owner Nobu Matsuhisa currently has 25 restaurants in 21 different cities around the world, spanning across five continents. Acclaimed actor, director, producer, and two-time Academy Award- winner Robert De Niro is a co-founder, instrumental in providing creative direction for all Nobu Restaurants. The menu offers cold dishes, hot dishes, tempura and kushiyaki, sushi and sashimi, and desserts. Off the cold menu, I love the yellowtail tartare with caviar and the oysters with Nobu sauces. My favorite hot dishes are the black cod with miso and the king crab tempura with amazu ponzu sauce. If you want to experience the true essence of Chef Nobu Matsuhisa's cuisine, I suggest his multicourse Omakase menu.

Osetra Seafood & Steaks, 904 5th Ave., San Diego, CA 92101; (619) 239-1800; osetraseafoodandsteaks.com; Seafood; $$$$. Taking great pride in supporting local seafood farmers, Osetra serves dinner nightly, offering a gourmet seafood menu along with "Wine Angels" (pretty girls) who fly to retrieve your fine wine selection from their extraordinary three-story collection. With culinary inspirations from Europe, the Americas, and the Pacific Rim, the menu offers some of the finest and freshest seafood around, as well as aged meats and homemade pastas. An impressive oyster bar offers local oysters, caviar, sashimi, shrimp cocktail, and more. Up to four types of oysters are offered daily, including Kumamoto oysters, kumai oysters, Bahia Falsa oysters, and, very rare, Huma Huma oysters. An ice bar offers an extensive collection of vodkas. Great choices off the new sushi menu include the Double Double Tuna Roll, Tempura Lobster Roll, or the Spicy Diego Roll.

Osteria Panevino, 722 5th Ave., San Diego, CA 92101; (619) 595-7959; osteriapanevino.com; Italian; $$$$. Experience fine Italian cuisine in a setting reminiscent of a small bistro dotting the hills of Firenze and the Tuscan region of Italy. Your meal is served in a farmhouse setting complete with terra-cotta floor tiles, large paintings and murals on the walls, colored tablecloths, and a full-marbled bar. Choose the intimate dining room or open-air patio where the Gaslamp pedestrians are shuffling along busy 5th Avenue. They operate a fine bakery producing fresh breads, pastas, and desserts daily. Be sure to review their extensive and award- winning wine list featuring a wide variety of California and Italian labels. Your entire meal could be spent tasting the many varieties of fresh mozzarellas available in the antipasti section, served in several savory presentations. The pasta menu is equally impressive. A great example is the strozzapreti emiliani, twisted pasta with roasted pork loin, Portobello mushrooms, and sun-dried tomatoes, tossed in a tomato sauce infused with rosemary. This is one eatery that will require multiple visits to sample the variety of offerings.

Richard Walker's Pancake House, 520 Front St., San Diego, CA 92101; (619) 231-7777; richardwalkers.com; American; $$. Imagine taking a bite out of a massive and sugary baked apple pancake with imported Saigon cinnamon and clarified butter! There's quite a bit more to like about this whimsical restaurant, cleverly decorated with stained- glass windows and hand-blown glass fixtures. An extensive menu of gourmet pancakes, waffles, crepes, and omelets are the stars here. First-time visitors beware of the long lines, especially on the weekends, but hang in there, the "wow factor" when the food arrives at your table is worth the wait. The blueberry and sour cream crepes are pure comfort. Richard Walker, who owns and operates two larger pancake houses in Illinois, refers to his San Diego restaurant in the Marina District as "the little diamond of downtown." There's also seating on a busy outdoor patio. Additional location is at 909 Prospect St, La Jolla, CA 92037.

Royal India, 329 Market St., San Diego, CA 92101; (619) 269-9999; royalindia.com; Middle Eastern; $$$. With awards including "Best Indian" and "Most Romantic Restaurant" in San Diego, there is no doubt that Royal India sets the standard for San Diego's Indian cuisine. Royal India treats its guests like royalty with its richly colored and plush architectural design in a tranquil setting complete with imported items directly from the palaces of India, including the royal chandeliers that dangle above a custom-carved wood bar. A diverse and assorted menu focuses on home-cooked family recipes that incorporate fresh herbs and spices with top-quality vegetables, seafood, and meats. I highly recommend the spicy tandoori wings and the chicken coconut pineapple curry. Multiple locations can be found throughout San Diego.

Sally's Fish House & Bar, 1 Market Place, San Diego, CA 92101; (619) 358-6740; sallyssandiego.com; Seafood; $$$$. "Where Passion Meets the Plate" is the slogan at Sally's. Bordering Seaport Village, this modern-looking restaurant, decked out with high ceilings, numerous windows, and granite countertops, is further complemented with dark woods, black accents, and work from local artists adoring the walls. Grab a seat at one of the high-top tables with an up-close and personal view of the marina. The menu is seafood-dominated, with vibrant ocean flavors in every entrée— particularly the sushi and sashimi offerings. The Canadian lobster potpie is an irresistible marriage of pungent lobster with assorted seasonal veggies, linguica, and Boursin cheese, all underneath a blanket of puff pastry. The chili-crusted Maine diver scallops with preserved lemon raviolis, pine nut relish, and a velvety white wine butter sauce gets equal billing. A 3-course prix-fixe menu that changes from week to week is another nice option. Reservations are strongly recommended.

STK San Diego, 600 F St, San Diego, CA 92101; (619) 354-5988; togrp.com; Steakhouse; $$$$. STK San Diego at the Andaz Hotel in the Gaslamp District offers the fine dining experience of a traditional steakhouse paired with a chic lounge. A sleek, contemporary design and in-house DJ creates an infectious, high-energy vibe. The menu features reimagined classic American cuisine with signature dishes and world-class service.

The Kebab Shop, 303 W. Beech St., Suite C-2, San Diego, CA 92101; (619) 550-5481; thekebabshop.com; Middle Eastern; $$. A.J. Break away from your daily routine and escape to this European getaway offering a delectable array of healthy and authentic options including Turkish Döner kebabs, originally from Turkey, offered in spiced lamb, marinated chicken, or falafel with a mix of fresh vegetables, a creamy garlic yogurt sauce, and homemade spicy sauce. Choose from shawarma sandwiches on soft, fluffy rolls, and sides including hot French fries and saffron rice. Other popular favorites include shish kebab plates, rotisserie plates, and Iskender kebab (rarely found in the US). A selection of fresh salads includes the Bebe Caprese, Tabouli, and Algerian Eggplant salad. Multiple locations can be found throughout San Diego.

The Oceanaire Seafood Room, 400 J St., San Diego, CA 92101; (619) 858-2277; theoceanaire.com; Seafood; $$$$. The Oceanaire Seafood Room lives up to its name by offering only the finest and freshest sustainably caught seafood from prompt and professional servers. With its sprawling, dark-wood dining room and tables adorned in white linen, you'll feel as if you've stepped back in time to a classic 1930s ocean liner. A sizeable menu provides regionally inspired and seasonal offerings that are based on market availability. Fish is flown in daily from around the world, and one of the most famous items on the menu is the baked Maryland blue crab cake. California Dover sole emerges from the oven stuffed with spinach, blue crab, and shrimp, and the classic beer-battered fish-and-chips is deep-fried to a light and golden crunch on the outside, yet tender and juicy inside. The prosciutto- wrapped Scottish Loch Duart salmon with roasted red pepper relish is wildly delicious. Seasoned wine stewards are always on hand to answer questions and help you chart a course for the wine selection that best complements your meal.

Westgate Room, 1055 2nd Ave., San Diego, CA 92101; (619) 238-1818; westgatehotel.com; French; $$$$. Built over 40 years ago, the Westgate Hotel has an elegant interior and decor reminiscent of French nobility. Executive Chef Fabrice Hardel of the award-winning Westgate Room is consistently pleasing diners with his creative and delicate gourmet French cuisine offered in a graceful and European- inspired atmosphere. Staying away from the old-world style of creating French cuisine, Hardel has left heavy cream and butter behind for a new lease on lighter fare. For lunch try the milk-fed veal picatta with Yukon potato gnocchi or the Alaskan halibut cheeks with sweet yellow corn risotto. Start your evening with a creative cocktail from the Plaza Bar and relax and unwind with live entertainment. The dinner menu changes with the seasons to take advantage of the freshest ingredients. A few of the most popular year-round items include British Columbia king salmon,

Black Angus beef tenderloin with German butterball potato, and Colorado lamb chop mascarpone polenta. The dessert menu is a special creation that exudes indulgence. Two of my favorites are the fragrant Tonka Bean Crème Brulee and creamy Honeycomb Panna Cotta.

National City, Chula Vista, La Mesa & El Cajon

This area of San Diego is large and diverse, spanning much of the south-coastal communities between San Diego and Mexico and stretching to the easternmost borders of the county. Primarily settled by ranchers in the 1800s, this area was also frequented by workers traveling between San Diego and gold mining operations in the mountains. Major growth was seen in these communities after World War II in the 1940s and '50s.

National City is home to a 3-mile port area along the San Diego Bay, including the Naval Base San Diego, one of the largest US Naval bases on the west coast. One of the first "auto malls" ever built in the world is located on a strip dubbed "the Mile of Cars," and Highland Avenue is considered one of the more popular cruising routes for auto enthusiasts. Listed as a California Historical Landmark, the National City Depot was built in 1882 and served as the first Pacific Coast terminus station of the Santa Fe Railway system's transcontinental railroad. Also, a large attraction for South County residents is the Westfield Plaza Bonita shopping mall, which includes a large cinema complex and plenty of unique and chain department stores.

Chula Vista earned its name due to the scenic location between San Diego Bay and coastal mountain foothills. It is the second largest city in San Diego County, and home to one of Americas few year-round US Olympic Training centers. Other popular tourist destinations include a large outdoor amphitheater used for concerts year-round and Knott's Soak City USA. A large marina is home to the Chula Vista Yacht Club, and sports fishing and whale watching charters operate daily. The Nature Center is home to interactive exhibits describing geologic and historic aspects of the

169

Sweetwater Marsh and San Diego Bay. The Center has exhibits on sharks, rays, water birds, birds of prey, insects, and flora. El Cajon is located in the eastern portion of the county, along the I-8 corridor between San Diego and the Cleveland National Forest. Several interesting museums call El Cajon home, including the San Diego Aero-Space Museum and Heritage of the Americas. A number of popular golf courses are open daily. Both Sycuan and Viejas Indian Reservations and casinos border the eastern end, and attract professional and casual gamblers alike.

Anthony's Fish Grotto, 9530 Murray Dr., La Mesa, CA 91942; (619) 463-0368; anthonysfishgrotto.com; Seafood; $$$. For more than 70 years, Anthony's Fish Grotto has been pleasing multiple generations of regulars. Kids who once dined in diapers are returning with their own families. It's no surprise that they're voted one of the best seafood restaurants in San Diego. Located in a scenic area with a beautiful man-made lake in the background, you can choose a seat with a view. The lobby is decorated like an underwater paradise, complete with rock walls and plenty of fish seemingly floating in the air. Here you will find the freshest seasonal catches, including shrimp, crab, albacore tuna, cod, sole, and more. The most popular items are their oyster shooters, creamy clam chowder, and crispy calamari. I love the crab stuffed mushrooms and Crab Louis salad, but the fresh catches of the day are always a sure bet. They also have a full-service fish market.

The Barbecue Pit, 920 E. Plaza Blvd., National City, CA 91950; (619) 477-2244; Barbecue; $$. Established in San Diego over 60 years ago, the Texas-style recipes have been handed down for generations. The interior hasn't changed much over the years, with plenty of wood throughout the dining room and animal heads hanging on the walls. You simply order your meal at the front, then sit at the communal tables and enjoy some of the best barbecue in town. Nothing fancy here, just a large selection of timeless favorites at an extremely reasonable price. The sauce is a blend of flavors, ranging from savory to sweet, with just the right tang to tickle your taste buds. Obviously, the chicken and ribs are the most popular items, but I really enjoyed the ham dinner with coleslaw, potato salad, and old-fashioned baked beans. The sliced barbecue beef sandwich is also an excellent choice. This is a great choice for catering a business gathering or special occasion. Additional location is at 2390 Fletcher Pkwy, El Cajon, CA 92020. Additional locations throughout San Diego.

Cafe La Maze, 1441 Highland Ave., National City, CA 91950; (619) 474-3222; cafelamaze.com; Steak House; $$$. This legendary restaurant has been serving locals and visitors for over 70 years. Best of all, they've kept the interior reminiscent of the Golden Era of Hollywood, with comfortable booths and decor that will make you feel like you're dining in a classic 1940s and '50s era steak house. During the Prohibition years, many of Hollywood's elite would travel to Tijuana for gambling at the Caliente racetrack, but the trek was significantly longer than our modern times, as interstate highways were only beginning to take shape. Marcel Lamaze, a legendary and influential restaurateur and maître d' in Los Angeles, was challenged by his connections to establish a halfway house near the Mexican border, as a pit stop for rest (and gambling). All of Marcel's acquaintances still adorn the walls, and take you back to an influential and entertaining time in American history. Cafe La Maze's famous prime rib steak is still the most popular dish on the menu today, but many seafood selections are also tempting to the palate. And unlike recent trends at most fine dining restaurants, all meals still include a choice of soup or salad, seasonal vegetables, and a starch. Open daily for lunch and dinner, oftentimes with live music in the evenings.

Cali Comfort BBQ, 8910 Troy St., Spring Valley, CA 91977; (619) 337-0670; calicomfortbbq.com; Barbecue $$. If you love barbecued food, this is the place to have it! A hidden gem in East County, Cali Comfort BBQ is a great hangout for food and fun. They smoke their meats the "low-n-slow" traditional way in their Ole Hickory Smoker with select California cooking woods. Their special Cali Dry Rubs add a one of a kind flavor that can't be beat. Popular favorites include the Pork Ribs that are smoked for six hours and lightly basted in BBQ sauce, and the Southern Mac n' Cheese with crispy bacon, blackened chicken, and sour cream. Don't miss the Tri-Tip Cheese Steak Sandwich with melted provolone, and grilled peppers and onions served on a torpedo roll; add a grilled jalapeño for some extra heat!

Casa de Pico, 5500 Grossmont Center Dr., La Mesa, CA 92142; (619) 463-3267; casadepico.com; Mexican; $$. Take part in the true spirit of Mexico by tasting regional and traditional food in a colorful dining room with hand-painted artwork and wrought-iron chandeliers. A heated patio offers a fountain, tropical plants and colorful flowers, frosty margaritas, and strolling mariachis. This is certainly not the right place for a quiet, romantic interlude! This location is perfect for a family or office gathering where you're looking for plenty of entertainment. Their handmade tortillas are served warm off the griddle and prepared for you right in the front lobby area. Be sure to try their most popular item, the Cheese Crisp Special, a crisp flour tortilla topped with refried beans, two kinds of beef or shredded chicken and melted cheese, avocado slices, tomato wedges, guacamole, and sour cream. It's been on the menu for over 40 years!

D.Z. Akins, 6930 Alvarado Rd., San Diego, CA 92120; (619) 265-0218; dzakinsdeli.com; American; $$. Since 1980, D.Z. Akins has expanded their restaurant five times to accommodate diners clambering at their door for down-home, New York–style deli food in massive portions. Open at 7 a.m. for breakfast daily; choose from 3 dozen selections including French toast, Belgian waffles, omelets, steak and eggs, smoked salmon (lox), and more. For lunch, the menu boasts 134 unique sandwiches, including Triple-Deckers, piled sky-high with top quality deli meats such as corned beef, pastrami, turkey, and roast beef. Complete dinner entrees include historical favorites like corned beef and cabbage, roast brisket of beef, and stuffed cabbage rolls. Old-fashioned desserts include sundaes, shakes, malts, and sodas. They say they make the best cheesecake in San Diego . . . guess what, they are right!

Giardino Neighborhood Cucina, 8131 Broadway Lemon Grove, CA 91945; (619) 825-7112; giardinosd.com; Italian; $$. Experience a taste of Italy at Giardino Neighborhood Cucina, a true family-owned and operated restaurant in Lemon Grove. A small private room in the back of the restaurant, where the pasta is made, is also available for intimate events and celebrations. One of the most unique items on the menu is the Chefs Pizza. The Steak Siciliano is another favorite. The menu changes seasonally, is made from fresh and local products, namely from Lemon Grove farmers.

Hans & Harry's Bakery, 5080 Bonita Rd., Bonita, CA 91902; (619) 475-2253; hans-harry.com; Bakery; $$. Since 1991, customers have been raving about the gourmet cakes, strudels, and pastries from this retail bakery in Bonita. Trained in the fine art of European cake design and baking in their native country of Holland, business partners and skilled Pastry Chefs Hans Zandee and Harry Eijsermans have been luring customers to their bakery for an assortment of elaborate confections made with the finest and freshest ingredients available. Combining over 5 decades of experience, they have been able to achieve the best of the Old-World European cake styles, with the current creations of quality crafted cakes. Today, they are still hard at work putting their finishing touches on one-of-a-kind, sugary masterpieces. Surprise the chocolate lover in your life with a Belgian chocolate truffle cake, walnut fudge brownies, or a Black Forest strudel. Hans and Harry will inspire you to try all of their creations— just not in one visit of course!

Luna Grill, 2275 Otay Lakes Rd., Ste. 119, Chula Vista, CA 91914; (619) 656-5862; lunagrill.com; Middle Eastern; $$. Make a better fast food choice at Luna Grill, where eating on the go can be a healthy and affordable experience. Specializing in Near East and Mediterranean cuisine, the menu focuses on grilled-to-order kabobs. They offer all-natural beef, lamb, and poultry paired with marinades and dressings made from scratch daily. There are also plenty of vegan and vegetarian choices to satisfy any craving. A couple of excellent starters include the spicy cilantro hummus with whole-wheat flatbread, or traditional Persian Eggplant dip with pita bread, and topped with yogurt and sautéed mint. Or try their traditional spanakopita: baked phyllo dough filled with spinach and feta cheese. All of the kebabs can be served in a sandwich, as a salad topping, or as an entrée with basmati rice, pita bread, cucumber yogurt dip, fresh green salad, and a grilled tomato or carrots. Multiple locations can be found throughout San Diego.

Ono's Cafe, 4154 Bonita Rd., Bonita, CA 91902; (619) 470-6667; onoscafe.com; Islands; $$. Ono's Cafe offers an Asian Fusion, Pacific Rim cuisine with Hawaiian and Filipino influences. Located in a mall near the Chula Vista Municipal Golf Course, this restaurant has limited seating inside and additional tables on the outdoor patio. Prominent Hawaiian decorations will greet you, including a large tiki and 750-gallon fish tank as a centerpiece. Well-known for their sushi, they also offer plenty of other seafood and chicken options. One of their best specialty rolls is the Onolicious, with smoked salmon, crab, and cream cheese deep-fried in tempura batter. Two excellent entrees include the Seafood Dynamite; a little tower served on top of rice with a soy vinaigrette salad, and the macadamia nut-crusted salmon with unique cranberry coleslaw. But the best-kept secret is the Malasaza—a Portuguese doughnut-sweetbread baked to order with sugar or cinnamon.

Romesco Mexiterranean Bistro, 4346 Bonita Rd., Bonita, CA 91902; (619) 475-8627; romescomexmed.com; Mexican; $$. Enjoy traditional Mexican fare on a whole new level, at this happening bistro. The main dining room is subdued and relaxing, or you can choose the separated tapas bar that's open late and is much livelier. In either case, you're sure to enjoy a meal that will tantalize your senses. The tapas menu is extensive, making your decisions more difficult, but the staff is happy to understand your tastes and make appropriate recommendations. For dinner, the lamb asada is a colorful and amazingly complex mixture of flavors. Mediterranean specialties include the beef Milanesa Napolitana, a lightly breaded steak stuffed with ham and mozzarella and topped with marinara. Even the wine and craft beer lists highlight the Baja area, although there are plenty of other options to suit your taste.

San Diego Chicken Pie Shop, 2633 El Cajon Blvd., San Diego, CA 92104; (619) 295-0156; chickenpieshops.com; American; $$. What was started in 1938 by owner George B. Whitehead as a tiny eatery on the corner of Fifth and Robinson Avenues in Hillcrest has moved not once but twice to accommodate demand. The current location in North Park on El Cajon Boulevard is definitely big enough for everyone to enjoy old-fashioned chicken pie and gravy. The inside dining room is not fancy by any means, offering a laid-back country-style atmosphere with plain wooden tables and chairs and old photos and memorabilia adorning the walls. The chicken pie dinner is a dirt-cheap deal served with soup, salad, coleslaw, mashed potatoes and gravy, veggies, warm roll, and a slice of pie for dessert. Take one of the delicious homemade pies with you! Great choices include blueberry, peach, lemon, coconut and pineapple cream. This home- style restaurant with a come-back-soon hospitality offers food a la carte as well as a take-out menu. No checks, no credit cards, no debit cards. It has been a cash- only business since the beginning.

Sammy's Woodfired Pizza & Grill, 8555 Fletcher Pkwy. La Mesa, CA 91942; (619) 460-8555; sammyspizza.com; Pizza; $$. Known for its award-winning gourmet pizzas, tapas, salads, and pastas, Sammy's menu is constantly evolving and expanding with unique dishes and an expansive gluten-free menu that caters to a wider audience. Sammy's conveys a healthy, fresh, and organic approach with dishes including the tabouli and quinoa salad, featuring organic cucumber, parsley, mint, red onion, tomato, carrot, lemon juice, extra-virgin olive oil, and romaine. Or try the Redwood Hill Farms smoked goat cheddar artisan thin-crust pizza, made with oven-roasted tomatoes and fresh organic rosemary. A new vegan menu keeps ingredients fresh and light with delicious selections that exclude meat, eggs, dairy products, and all other animal-derived ingredients. Appetizing items include tapas such as the oak- roasted asparagus with vegan mozzarella, extra-virgin olive oil, and balsamic vinegar, various salads with dressings made from scratch, and delicious pizzas made on whole-wheat or gluten-free crust with dairy- free mozzarella. Sammy's also adds sophistication to its dessert menu with salted butterscotch pudding and orange-infused whipped cream. Multiple locations can be found throughout San Diego.

Surf Rider Pizza Co., 8381 La Mesa Blvd. La Mesa, CA 91942; (619) 340-1270; surfrider.pizza Pizza; $$. Think thin and crispy East Coast style pizza made with homemade hand tossed dough and whole milk mozzarella, all baked in fire heated brick ovens. Surf Rider Pizza Co. was founded by a true East Coast native with the goal of spreading pizza goodness to the West Coast. Surf Rider also offers fresh salads, authentic Stromboli and cheesesteaks, decadent homemade desserts, and craft beer. Also located in Ocean Beach.

Terra American Bistro, 7091 El Cajon Blvd., San Diego, CA 92115; (619) 293-7088; terrasd.com; American; $$$. Boasting a bar in the shape of a horseshoe and a captivating chandelier over the chef's communal farm table, this cozy New American bistro reverberates with a style all its own. The restaurant decor offers warm colors of tan and brown, with brick, wooden beams and polished concrete. Executive Chef-Owner Jeff Rossman offers a seasonal menu, focused on local, organic, and sustainable ingredients, even pulling herbs off his wall garden from time to time. Homemade soup of the day may include anything from white chili bean to vegetable bisque or seafood chowder. Flatbread pizzas and ginger chicken pot stickers are great to share. Build your own burger or opt for the barbecue sliders, which may seem small, but are extremely filling. Great lobster options include the lobster BLT with smoked bacon or the lobster macaroni n' cheese. Grilled yellowtail or rock cod are some of the fresh catches of the day that you may find here. One more thing—don't miss the pumpkin ravioli! Terra welcomes vegan, vegetarian, and gluten-free guests. Rossman's cookbook, From Terra's Table: New American Food, Fresh from Southern California's Organic Farms, is the recipient of several awards.

The Morning After, 531 F St, San Diego, CA 92101; (619) 542-9664; themorningaftersd.com; Breakfast; $$. Answering the call for a fun and social breakfast, brunch and lunch in the Gaslamp Quarter, this 4,132-square-foot bistro and bar creates colorful, whimsical dishes and drinks with flair in the early morning, and transitions to a sports bar in the evening. Think Fruity Pebbles pancakes topped with mascarpone buttercream for breakfast and buffalo wings, mac 'n cheese, or a buttermilk chicken and waffle plate for dinner.

TJ Oyster Bar, 4246 Bonita Rd., Bonita, CA 91902; (619) 267-4577; Seafood; $$. Started over 30 years ago on a corner in Tijuana, Mexico, the current location continues with the same traditional-style menu that made the business so popular. Don't let the diminutive size fool you, as the menu includes some heavy-hitting favorites that make this place a popular hangout for many of the locals, as well as the astute readers who circulate the positive reputation. Clearly, oysters on the half shell are a signature item, but don't pass by the unique flavors of the aguachile en molcajete, a bowl of raw shrimp drowned in lemon juice and hot chilies to create a ceviche, and served with onions and cucumbers. Other traditional favorites include smoked marlin or stingray tacos, and a whole fried fish that has a crispy crust and tender meat. Now with three locations including Chula Vista.

Bonus Chapter: Foodie Day Trips

Whether you're just visiting our fair city or call San Diego home, be sure to broaden your horizons beyond our county lines. This chapter highlights several places to spend a day or weekend away from the routine. Each destination has its own unique charm and is within an hour's drive, which makes it easy to navigate. Most important, they all offer enough activities to keep you occupied, whether you're young or old, alone or with a large family. We would strongly recommend planning an overnight stay to maximize your adventure. Here you will find a Wild Western town situated among soaring mountain pine forests, a warm valley with endless rows of grapevines and citrus groves, a posh seaside resort frequented by the Hollywood elite, and an island retreat accessible only by boat or helicopter. Expand your horizons and enjoy the diversity!

Julian

For a historical day trip near San Diego, there's no better destination than Julian. Located approximately 1 hour east of San Diego in the pine and oak wooded mountains, Julian offers visitors a chance to step back into the Wild West. This small town was originally founded in the late 1800s as a centerpiece to the gold rush. One of the first mining claims in this area was filed in February 1870. Soon after, the town grew quickly to accommodate the many settlers looking for a better life. Today, it is considered the premier mountain retreat in San Diego County, and one of the rare local areas with distinct four seasons. In the spring, you'll find meadows of blossoming flowers including daffodils. The summer is very warm and a perfect location for hiking, camping, picnicking, and stargazing. The cooler months of fall announce the beginning of apple harvest, one of the most recognizable attractions to this town. Winter days and nights are cool and crisp, with light snowfalls common between November and February. Where else could you snow sled in the morning and surf that same afternoon? The town center is only a few blocks long, and looks much like an old western settlement. Specialty shops feature handmade jewelry, antiques, artwork, and plenty of souvenirs. There are over 20 restaurants, a number of historic locations, and plenty of lodging choices, including bed & breakfast, lodges, cottages, and traditional hotels.

Visiting in the spring and fall months is especially nice when the foliage is just blooming or fruit is at the peak of harvest. Breakfast at the **Julian Cafe and Bakery** (2112 Main St.; 760-765-2712) is comfort food at its best. The chicken-fried steak and eggs, smothered in creamy gravy, with hash browns, homemade biscuits and jam, and coffee can last you all day. For lunch, a great stop is the **Miner's Diner** (2134 Main St.; 760-765-3753). Although they have a full menu for breakfast and lunch, the centerpiece is a sit-down bar with an old-fashioned soda fountain; a perfect place to rest your tired feet and enjoy a pick-me-up for the rest of the day. For dinner, try the **The Rongbranch Restaurant** (2722 Washington St.; (760) 765-2265), featuring their famous made from scratch chicken pot pie or hand-breaded and deep-fried dill pickles served with homemade ranch dressing. Don't miss the chicken, beef, or pork ribs served with their own special Bumsteer BBQ Sauce, plus great burgers, sandwiches, and more.

©*Maria Desiderata Montana*

There are three main bakeries in town, all located on Main Street. **Apple Alley Bakery** (2122 Main St.; 760-765-2532; facebook.com/AppleAlleyBakery) serves a variety of homemade apple pies, pastries, and cookies. They also have a great lunch menu. **Julian Pie Company** (2225 Main St.; 760-765-2449; julianpie.com) is a locally owned family business specializing in apple pies and cider   doughnuts. They source their apples from nearly 17,000 local trees and serve delicious pies and pastries at both their Julian and Santa Ysabel locations. **Mom's Pies** (2119 Main St.; 760-765-2472; momspiesjulian.com) has a large front window on Main Street where visitors can watch bakers prepare pies and baked goods throughout the day. Lunch is also available. If you plan to visit any of these proprietors, keep in mind that the lines for pies can get extremely long during Apple Harvest Season. Consider making the trip during the off-season or during the weekday.

Nearby you can visit a number of local wineries, as well as tour an inactive gold mine. Recreational gold panning continues to this day in a small area east of town called Banner Creek. There are also plenty of self-picking orchards available during the season. See the **Julian Chamber of Commerce** website for more information (julianca.com/index).

There are three major routes to access Julian. The northern access is via SR 76/SR 79, which links to northern San Diego and southwestern Riverside Counties, including routes to I-15. SR 78 comes to Julian from the west, providing access to Ramona and Escondido, and continues down the eastern slope of the mountains to SR 86 in Imperial County. The southern access is SR 79 through Cuyamaca Rancho State Park, which ultimately intersects with I-8.

If you choose to access Julian from the west on SR 78, be sure to make a pit stop at a landmark located in Santa Ysabel, at the intersection with SR 79. The now famous **Dudley's Bakery** (30218 CA 78, Santa Ysabel; 760-765-0488; dudleysbakery.com) was founded in 1963 and continues to have a loyal following. At the time it was established, many thought the expert baker Dudley Pratt was making a huge mistake, as Santa Ysabel was too far from San Diego and its neighboring communities. Nearly 50 years later, this small bakery continues to draw customers from all parts of the county. They serve over 40 different types of breads, fruit bars, and pastries (try the cinnamon raisin and Baja jalapeño breads). All of their items are also available online or at many grocery stores throughout San Diego.

Temecula

Located in the southwest portion of Riverside County, Temecula is approximately a 1-hour drive from many points near San Diego. Prior to the discovery of this area by Spanish missionaries in 1798, it is believed that the Pechanga Band of Luiseño Indians lived here for hundreds of years. After the Mexican-American War, many settlers began arriving in the area. This was the location for the second established post office in the entire state of California.

Primarily recognized for its burgeoning wine industry, Temecula is a major draw for visitors from both the southern San Diego areas, as well as many points north, Orange County, Riverside, Los Angeles, and Palm Springs. The most rapid growth was seen in the 1990s, when families were drawn by the affordable housing prices and warm climate. The major route into Temecula is using I-15, both north and south.

On the western end of the town, you will find Old Town Temecula, a collection of historic 1890s buildings within a walkable few blocks along Front Street. Here you will enjoy browsing through many antiques stores and dealers, specialty food stores, art galleries, boutiques and gift shops. The Temecula Museum features exhibits about the local band of Native Americans, local natural history, and city development. A number of themed restaurants and bars are available for dining and nighttime entertainment. Hot air balloon rides and horseback riding are also very popular.

The first commercial wine grapes were planted in the 1960s, and the area now boasts over 35 wineries, with many more under construction. Spread over 35,000 acres of rolling hills and vineyards, you can easily spend a day tasting the many varietals available. The climate is perfect for growing Chardonnay, Merlot, and Sauvignon Blanc. In recent years, wineries have also begun producing Mediterranean varietals like Viognier, Syrah, and Pinot Gris. The hotter temperatures are also particularly well suited to grapes such as the Rhône varietals, Cabernet Sauvignon, and Zinfandel.

Wine tasting is available at most of the wineries on a daily basis, as well as informative winery tours and large winery events, especially near harvest season. Along with remarkable wines, you'll also find excellent restaurants located in or near the wineries. The **Pinnacle Restaurant at Falkner Winery** (40620 Calle Contento; 951-676-8231; falknerwinery.com) includes sweeping views of the Temecula Valley and vineyards and specializes in daily Mediterranean-style cuisine. There's a BBQ picnic on Sundays. The **Creekside Grille at Wilson Creek Winery** (5960 Rancho California Rd.; 951-699-9463; wilsoncreekwinery.com) offers spacious dining both inside and outside, with a focus on California Modern cuisine. **Baily's Fine Dining** is located in Old Town Temecula (28699 Front St.; 951-676-9567; baily.com) and offers dining at two distinct restaurants specializing in California Continental and American Modern cuisines.

If you choose to stay for more than 1 day, there are a number of intimate bed-and-breakfast inns and larger resorts to call home. The accommodations at the **South Coast Winery Resort & Spa** (34843 Rancho California Rd., Temecula; 951-587-9463; wineresort.com) are luxurious. Each villa room opens to a small patio and breathtaking views of the surrounding vineyards. Since there are no common walls between villas, it's like having your own private residence in paradise. The well-recognized spa is an oasis of relaxation. No visit would be complete without lunch or dinner at its award- winning **Vineyard Rose Restaurant**. The atmosphere during a warm summer night on the patio is beautiful. Candlelight and a great bottle of wine make this one of the more romantic getaways in Southern California.

Laguna Beach

Located halfway to Los Angeles, this seaside resort city is approximately a 1-hour drive from San Diego. From the south, you can reach Laguna Beach using Pacific Coast Highway 1, which intersects with I-5 near Dana Point. PCH 1 also continues north to Newport Beach and the south Los Angeles area. From the east, you can utilize SR 133, which intersects with SR 73 (toll road) near Aliso Viejo. It is one of the premier destinations for visitors in southern California, with 20 sandy beaches and coves available for oceanfront recreation, including surfing, sunbathing, and swimming. Nearby you can catch a catamaran for whale and dolphin watching excursions.

What once started as a small community of artists looking for a home away from the busy Los Angeles city life is now home to more than 100 art galleries, studios, and boutiques. The city has more than 65 unique works of public art, designed and created specifically for Laguna Beach, including murals, statues, benches, and more. The **Laguna Art Museum** (lagunaartmuseum.org) is one of the oldest in the state and focuses on the cultural heritage of California and the unique history of the local area. Open Mon, Tues, and Fri to Sun 11 a.m. to 5 p.m.; Thurs 11 a.m. to 9 p.m. Closed Wed.

Two large art fairs run during the summer months, although there are many other art-related events throughout the year. Started in 1965, the **Sawdust Art Festival** features over 200 local artists showcasing paintings, jewelry, ceramics, photographs, sculptures, art glass, and textiles native to the area. You can also engage in demonstrations and workshops, with entertainment and lots to eat and drink throughout the day. Open 10 a.m. to 10 p.m. daily from late June to Labor Day. The **International Art Show** is also a main summer event, featuring over 125 international juried artists and master craftsmen. This event offers visitors a chance to browse through booths of original watercolors, oils, photography, sculpture, ceramics, glass, and more. You can also meet and talk with the artists. Open from 10 a.m. to 11:30 p.m. in July and August. Over

70 restaurants are located in the area, ranging from casual street food to top-tier dining. **Las Brisas** (361 Cliff Dr.; 949-497-5434; lasbrisaslagunabeach.com), located in a landmark building first opened, as the Victor Hugo Inn in 1938, is now a very popular destination for upscale Mexican cuisine. Another great upscale choice is **Bourban Steak Orange County** (1 Monarch Beach Resort; 949-234-3318; michaelmina.net), located within the magnificent St. Regis Monarch Beach Resort, featuring American cuisine inspired by award-winning chef Michael Mina. For authentic Italian dining, try **Ti Amo Ristorante** (31727 Coast Highway; 949-499-5350; tiamolaguna.com) with its romantic interior and fabulous pasta choices.

For a special occasion, or if you just want to feel pampered, the **Montage at Laguna Beach** is an experience like no other. Perched on an oceanfront bluff with expansive views of the Pacific Ocean, this luxury beach resort is situated on 30 lushly landscaped acres. There is also a 20,000-square-foot indoor/outdoor oceanfront spa. The crown jewel of this resort is the award-winning **Studio**, a Craftsman-inspired building reminiscent of an elegant and charming beach cottage. Facing west over the Laguna bluffs, the doors and windows are often opened to panoramic views and pleasant ocean breezes. The California-influenced French cuisine and expansive wine list make this one of my preferred destinations. Located at 30801 Coast Hwy. Laguna Beach (949-715-6000; montagelagunabeach.com).

Catalina Island

Catalina Island is located about 22 miles south-southwest of Los Angeles across the Pacific Ocean. Two main ferries service the Island; Catalina Express (catalinaexpress.com) leaves from San Pedro, Long Beach, Newport Beach, and Dana Point, and the Catalina Flyer (catalinainfo.com) departs from Marina Del Rey. A one-way trip averages between 60 and 90 minutes, depending on the departure port. Some run more frequently than others, so it is important to plan ahead. The closest and most convenient option from San Diego is the Catalina Express in Dana Point, about a 1-hour drive north on I-5, exiting at Pacific Coast Highway 1 and following the signs to Dana Harbor. Helicopter service is also available at a steeper price, and only takes 15 minutes one-way.

The island itself is 22 miles long and 8 miles across at its greatest width. About a million tourists visit the island every year. The main destination is the town of Avalon, near the southeastern tip of the island. A vast majority of the tourist activities, lodging, and businesses are located in this area. Avalon was first developed as a resort destination in 1888 by George Shatto, who also built the first hotel and a pier to welcome guests. In 1919, chewing-gum mogul William Wrigley Jr. bought out controlling interest in the Santa Catalina Island Company and invested millions in preserving and promoting the island. It wasn't until 1975 that the island's interests were deeded to the Catalina Island Conservancy, an organization that Wrigley helped create. A smaller resort village called Two Harbors is located on the northern isthmus. Only one restaurant, general store, and hotel are located here.

The use of motor vehicles on the island is restricted, so most residents use golf carts and bicycles for transportation. Tourists can hire a taxi from Catalina Transportation Services, but can also rent bicycles and golf carts in Avalon. A long list of activities is available to experience the Island and its many wonders. A number of small motor tours leave daily for a long loop through the backcountry, allowing visitors to view native bison and other wildlife, as well as experiencing stunning views of the island bluffs, beaches, and ocean. Other popular choices are helicopter tours, fishing expeditions, parasailing, snorkeling and scuba diving, hiking, and camping.

It's recommended you stay at least one night on the Island. For a special experience, consider the **Inn on Mt. Ada** (398 Wrigley Road, Avalon; 310-510-2030; innonmtada.com). This historic site was once owned by the Wrigley family and has since been restored to a stunning hotel with panoramic views of the island and Pacific Ocean. Another excellent choice is the **Hotel Metropole** (205 Crescent Avenue, 310-510-1884; hotel-metropole.com), an upscale oceanfront hideaway located next to the central marketplace. Avalon is also the center for shopping and dining. Strolling along the streets will transport you to a small Mediterranean village, and is perfectly designed to make window-shopping enjoyable. You'll find clothing, jewelry, antiques, artwork, gift shops and boutiques, and plenty of souvenirs.

As you can imagine, there is a great mix of restaurants to choose from, including fine dining, casual, and fast food. There are also a number of excellent bakeries, ice cream shops, coffee houses, and even a few bars/nightclubs for entertainment. Several restaurants top the list based on quality of the food, as well as local popularity, reflected in their long-running establishment. **Antonio's Pizzeria & Cabaret** (230 Crescent Ave.; 310-510-0008; catalinahotspots.com) is located on the waterfront, and has a great selection of casual meals and excellent drinks. Seating is available both inside and on an open patio. The calzone pairs great with a cold beer. Surprisingly, they also have some of the best pancakes on the island. **Steve's Steakhouse** (417 Crescent Ave.; 310-510- 0333; StevesSteakhouse.com) is a perfect destination for a more upscale dinner, with beautiful harbor views and a robust selection of quality meats and seafood. The rack of lamb is a local favorite. For a traditional Mexican breakfast, lunch, or dinner, be sure to stop by **Mi Casita Mexican Restaurant** (111 Claressa Ave.; 310-510-1772. The carne asada and margaritas are a great ending to a long day of shopping.

Bonus Recipe: California Fish Tacos with Cabbage and Red Pepper Slaw

By Maria Desiderata Montana

INGREDIENTS

4 cups shredded green cabbage
2 red bell peppers, seeded and julienned
4 tablespoons California Olive Ranch extra virgin olive oil, plus extra for coating the grill
4 teaspoons apple cider vinegar
2 teaspoons lemon juice
2 teaspoons dried oregano
Salt and pepper, to taste
4-6 ounce Alaskan White Cod fillets
8 corn tortillas

DIRECTIONS

In a large bowl combine cabbage and peppers. Add California Olive Ranch extra virgin olive oil, vinegar, lemon juice, oregano and salt and pepper. Lightly toss and set aside.

Preheat grill or stovetop grill pan to medium-high heat and brush grill rack with California Olive Ranch extra virgin olive oil. Grill fish until cooked through, about 4-5 minutes on each side, more or less, depending on thickness. Remove fillets from grill and cut into small sections. (Each 6-ounce fillet will make 2 tacos)

Place corn tortilla on a plate and fill with a spoon of the green cabbage and red pepper slaw. Top with fish. Repeat with remaining ingredients. Serve immediately.

Index

D

E

F

G

Made in the USA
Columbia, SC
11 May 2020